POWERFUL CHANGES!

LEARN THE PROVEN PATH TO FINANCIAL FREEDOM AND HAPPINESS

John R. Burley
and Bryan K. Fergus

Published by:
Treasure Chest Unlimited

This publication is designed to educate and provide general information regarding the subject matter covered. However, laws and practices often vary from state to state and are subject to change. Because each factual situation is different, specific advice should be tailored to the particular circumstances. For this reason, the reader is advised to consult with his or her own advisor regarding that individual's specific situation.

The author has taken reasonable precautions in the preparation of this book and believes the facts presented in the book are accurate as of the date it was written. However, neither the author nor the publisher assume any responsibility for any errors or omissions. The author and publisher specifically disclaim any liability resulting from the use or application of the information contained in this book, and the information is not intended to serve as legal advice related to individual situations.

Published by Prosperity Training, Inc., 1135 Terminal Way Ste. 209
Reno, NV 89502, 1-800-561-8246

Visit our Web site at www.johnburley.com

Library of Congress Cataloging-in-Publication Data

Burley, John R.
Powerful Changes : the path to riches and happiness /
John R. Burley and Bryan K. Fergus.

     p. cm.
     ISBN 1-929238-16-9

1. Business 2. Personal Development. 3. Finance, Personal. 4. Investing.   5. Real Estate.
I. Bryan K. Fergus   II. Title.
Printed in Australia by Griffin Press

First Printing: June 2003
10   9   8   7   6   5   4   3   2   1

Cover Design by ImageSupport.com, llc
Book design by Kevin Stock / ImageSupport.com, llc

POWERFUL CHANGES!

LEARN THE PROVEN PATH TO FINANCIAL FREEDOM AND HAPPINESS

John R. Burley
and Bryan K. Fergus

Testimonials

I first met John and Bryan at a seminar in 2002. I went to the seminar hoping to learn how to be more successful with money, I left the seminar with the knowledge about how to be more successful in life. John is an incredibly passionate teacher who genuinely cares about his students and truly wants all of them to live a life of abundance. Bryan has a way of helping you see things in such a different way that forces you to challenge old limiting beliefs and opens doors to your future.

Tony Dean, Omaha, Nebraska USA

John and Bryan both place great emphasis on building a business with integrity. They have helped me expand my mind around concepts that were completely foreign. Now I approach each situation from a different direction and try to help every person affected by it. With this level of training, I am not tempted to seek solutions which undermine my integrity. I can serve investors, customers and myself with pride.

Donovan Pieterse, Syracuse, New York USA

I have attended the Boot Camp since 1999, several times as an instructor. Since my first Boot Camp my life has changed in a profound way. I have a new investment strategy that I am in control of and reaps me returns regardless of the economic swings. For the first time I feel that my financial future is solid, not only because I have a profitable real estate portfolio but because I have learned a system that I can duplicate in any area of the United States. John Burley's seminars have given me the courage to change my perspective and the support I needed to become a successful investor.

Marleen Geyen, St. Bonifacius, Minnesota USA

John Burley has given us the blueprint for our success, we followed his teaching and the results have been unbelievable. He is truly a remarkable person, he gives new meaning to the word Integrity in every way possible. He cares so much for his students, sharing a range of topics far to many to mention. John is an inspiration to be around.

We thank Bryan for his work with Powerful Changes which has helped us not only in our investing success but in new meaning for our relationships with our family, it has encouraged us in the teaching, to share so much with so many. A truly inspirational experience.

Wayne and Ros Bourke, Taree, NSW Australia

I left school at the age of 16 to be employed on a dairy farm. Living on the belief that if l worked hard l would become rich. After seventeen years of working seven day's a week l began to look for the reason why l was so poor. The inspiration came from listening to John Burley's tape set Blue Print for success. I then had the incentive to change my view's, my lifestyle and the drive to get to financial freedom. In April 2000 l attended John Burley's Boot Camp and to date have acquired over 110 properties with a monthly cash flow which has allowed myself, and my wife Tracey to retire from milking cow's and to be financially free. I owe much to John Burley for as a mentor he has given myself and family much more than just the opportunity of understanding and striving for long-term wealth. Meeting Bryan in 2001 was another milestone in my life. Bryan helped me to marry the reality of wealth with spirituality. This understanding is that the two really do go hand in hand. Now, I really now what "Good Stewardship of Money" means. Today I am a full time Level 5 Investor and when l am not growing my property portfolio l am spending TIME with my wife and two children.

Adrian Oakman Masterton, New Zealand

In November 2001, I met John in person, learning first hand that what he taught was actually real and possible. I immediately implemented a change in my money habits; my Automatic Investment Plan (AIP), debt reduction and reassessment of my charitable giving were given my first priority. I met Bryan Fergus in April 2002 at John's Advanced Investing Boot Camp in Phoenix. Bryan's "Spirituality of Wealth" gave me the assurance that it was okay for me to strive for this new lifestyle and still maintain the balance between God, family and financial freedom. My transformation into a successful Investor had begun. John and Bryan hadn't just provided me with the "how to" invest but rather they had developed my mind as an investor. I now see the world as a world of abundance instead of a world of scarcity, a world full of opportunities instead of a world full of fear.

Leonie Jackson Glenmore Park, NSW Australia

After meeting John Burley in September 2000 my business began to grow into something that today is considered a beautiful success. John taught ideas I'd never known, ideas that were not found in the books or curriculums of the schools I'd been to. I learned from John the importance of Investing Principles such as Lag and Taking Action. Also, the idea of investing and working with strict Integrity, an absolute must in John's world, has led to the abundant success of my business. I watched John walk his talk and have been inspired to do the same. What I didn't realize, and Bryan Fergus pointed out to me, was that this journey I am on is really "The Evolution of a Life Change" and that many who become successful experience virtually the same evolution. I am grateful to both John and Bryan for writing this book Powerful Changes so that myself and others can understand more about the metamorphosis we are going through.

Damion Lupo, Scottsdale, AZ   USA

John Burley, one of the greatest investor minds in the world, is a man of great integrity who gives unselfishly to others, to empower people so that they can take charge of their financial future. John gives all of himself to show others how to change their thought process, to become a possibility thinker and to get the most out of what life has to offer.

The first time I heard John speak, I was immediately impressed. John changed my paradigm about my business and empowered me to be able to become financially free within 12 months providing. I owe John and his family a debt of gratitude for their unconditional giving and support. I appreciate him more than he will ever know.

I recommend anyone who is looking to improve their financial standing to make use of the information John has to offer.

C. Bradley Simmons Perryville, Kentucky USA

John Burley and Bryan Fergus are two people I consider to be among my very best friends. John showed me how investing works. He gave me a system that allowed me to stay home with my family. Now he is pushing me to the next level. Bryan has helped me find meaning in this journey towards wealth and independence. As a spiritually minded person it is vitally important to understand what role faith plays in this game.

Troy and Lori Mann Tulsa, Oklahoma USA

I have known John now for almost one year and Bryan for just over 6 months. In this short time I have learned so much form them. Not only about finances but also about life, trust, friendships, integrity, loyalty, and spirituality to just name a few. I think that I have lived a life up until I met John of complete scarcity. Through the training I have received from John I now know that there is so much more available for me and also every one else in this world who is willing to learn. John and Bryan have also shown me the true meaning of wealth and this has nothing to do with the amount of money you have. It's more to do with what you have inside your heart and how you go about using it to help yourself and to help others.

Gregg Hooper Broome, Western Australia

This book is dedicated to my loving Family. To my wife, Shari, and my great children John, Jr. and Danielle. Thank you for your support and all the incredible times together.
– John R. Burley

I dedicate this book to my wife, Debi, who has been my constant companion through many changes in life, and my wonderful children, Tristen, Tess, and Timothy.
– Bryan K. Fergus

TABLE OF CONTENTS

Preface – A Message From John Burley xi

Introduction – The Power of Change 1

Chapter 1 – A Whole Lot Of Changing Going On! 11

Chapter 2 – Dissatisfied With Settling 27

Chapter 3 – Standing At The Crossroads of Life – 47
              The Trigger Event

Chapter 4 – There Must Be A Better Way 71

Chapter 5 – Knock And It Will Open! 91

Chapter 6 – Time To Take Off! 105

Chapter 7 – Putting Your System In Place 121

Chapter 8 – Perseverance – 133
              Letting "Lag" Assure Your Success

Chapter 9 – Getting Better 147

Chapter 10 – Four Keys To Powerful Changes 161

Chapter 11 – Breaking Through Barriers 175

Conclusion – Putting The Power of Change to Work 185

Acknowledgements 192

Preface

A Message From John Burley

Welcome to *Powerful Changes*!

Ever since I was very young, I had a strong desire to become financially successful. I began, as a youth, selling door-to-door. At the age of six, I even started hiring others to work for me. In my teens I started a sales company that had over 20 employees. There was no doubt that my desire to become financially successful was strong. However, my knowledge and understanding of the process of becoming rich was weak.

So, like so many others, I just kept putting my head down and plowing forward. I celebrated many victories, but suffered far more defeats. When you get right down to it, I was basically hoping that through hard work and determination I would stumble my way to success. Eventually I realized that my plan at the time was not going to work. Even if it did, it became apparent that the long hours, stress and frustration wouldn't really make it worthwhile. I knew in my heart that if I was ever to become financially free I was going to need help. I was going to have to start studying and learning from others who had already achieved success. Then I was going to have to apply what I learned.

So I did. I put myself on a life-long learning program. Over a period of ten years I diligently read books, listened to tapes, watched videos and attended seminars. I was striving to learn what the secrets of the rich were so that I could put those secrets or steps into action. The results were astounding. Once I figured out the system, I changed how I handled money. In a period of a few short years I was a multi-millionaire at the age of 32 and in a position to choose whether or not I ever wanted to work again.

I chose not to stop working, although I don't work as near as hard as I used to. Instead, I made the choice to do the two types of work that have always been the most rewarding for me: investing in real estate and teaching others how to become financially free and happy.

This focus has enabled me to teach tens of thousands of people from dozens of different countries. Through the years I have witnessed that while all people are very different and come from all walks of life, the ones who followed the step-by-step system that I taught them became financially free regardless of their background. As a result, I wrote my first book, the #1 International Best-Seller _Money Secrets of the Rich!_ This book taught people a sure-fire 7-step system that when followed would lead to financial freedom. It is a very hands-on book. It's not based on theory or academics. Instead, the steps spelled out in _Money Secrets of the Rich!_ come from real world experience and have helped so many people become financially free.

That leads me to where I am today. In personally working with tens of thousands of people and watching them become financially free and happy, I came to realize that the keys to success and personal fulfillment have very little to do with how smart people are, or how much education they have, or their personal background or even their upbringing. These factors had little to do with their ability to make the changes that they wanted to bring to their lives. No, the secret to making Powerful Changes involved something else entirely. It was really all about the ability of people to understand their emotions and psychology so that they could move forward through the action steps required.

After observing thousands of students and then scientifically interviewing many of them (many of whom you will meet in this book), Bryan Fergus and I came to clearly realize that there are actually phases and steps that everyone can apply in order to create Powerful Changes in their lives. In this book you will have the opportunity to learn and apply the Step-By-Step System to achieve Financial Freedom and Happiness that we developed. Yes, you can learn these 8 Steps to Powerful Changes by reading the book that you hold in your hands.   I assure you that when you apply these 8 Steps they will empower you to experience the same type of success as you will read about in the real life stories contained in *Powerful Changes*! Thousands have already applied these steps and succeeded. You can too!

I am proud of you for beginning your trip down the path to financial freedom and happiness. Let *Powerful Changes*! serve as your guide.

As a way to give back to my Maker and to all who have supported and followed my works over the many years, my family and I have decided that all my proceeds and royalties from the book *Powerful Changes*! will go to charities that help, improve, and change the world for the better.

And again, as we begin this journey together for the changes that you need in your life I want to personally thank you for your determination and congratulate you on your success!

Powerful Changes! to you,

John R. Burley

Introduction

The Power of Change

An old familiar phrase tells us that there are only two certainties in life: death and taxes. That old familiar phrase needs to be revised to reflect real life in the twenty first century. It should go something like this: "There are three certainties in life: death, taxes, and change!" Change is a part of our lives. It happens everyday. Our world is in a constant state of change. We don't have to look very far to see evidence of that all around us.

Take technology for example. Technological pioneers tell us that the rate and progress of technology doubles every year. In other words, people are doubling the speed of twice as many innovative advances every year. What does that mean for real people living real lives? It means that the new computer that someone bought last weekend will be out of date twice as fast as the computer someone else bought last year. It means that the cutting edge cell phone of today will look like a dinosaur a year from now. It means that the home theatre system that someone painstakingly put together in a new home will need an upgrade before its owner ever figures out how to use the remote control!

Change isn't just taking place in the realm of technology. It's happening all over the world. Political decisions are made everyday that will alter the course and destiny of our world. Geographical boundaries will shift and new systems of government will come into existence that will reflect the changing dreams and wishes of the people of Planet Earth. As evidence of worldwide change, one American map company now offers an upgradeable globe program for its customers. Here's how it works: If you buy a globe of the world today and nations change names or geographical boundaries, the purchase price of your globe will be credited toward the purchase of a new globe! Worldwide change is simply part of the fabric that makes up life in the twenty first century.

Change is truly a universal and powerful force that impacts all of our lives. Our world is in a constant state of flux driven along by the power of change. What if you could harness the powerful force of change and put it to work for you? What if, instead of being tossed about by the waves of change, you could actually ride those waves toward the shoreline of a better life? If you could understand the process of change and put it to work for you, what would you do with your days? What would you become? What would your life look like?

John Burley faced these questions in the late 1980's. John knew that even though he was successful in the eyes of the business community, something needed to change in his life. He wasn't satisfied with the way he was spending his days. That thought would have surprised many of John's friends. From their perspective, John was a guy who had it all. From the time John was a child, he had a financial mind geared for business. As a young boy, John was out knocking on doors in his neighborhood selling cherry plumbs. At the age of six, in one summer John turned a profit of five hundred dollars. That was five hundred dollars free and clear after paying his employees and covering his supply costs. Yes, you read that right. John Burley was a six-year-old boy who had the brains to hire employees and to understand profits and losses. When John began winning sales awards in his late teens and outperforming people more than twice his age, he knew that he could make a good living in the business world.

John did make a good living in the business world. In his early twenties John took the path that most of his friends expected him to take. He jumped into the rat race of corporate America and began to achieve financial success. John became a successful financial planner with a very good income. He had what many people would consider the American dream. John had a nice home in an upscale neighborhood, a flashy car, his own financial planning practice, and the lifestyle to prove it. Many people would be content with that kind of life, but John knew that something was missing.

More than a flashy car, a nice home, and a successful business, John wanted his freedom. John wanted to be able to do what he wanted to do when he wanted to do it. Much to John's surprise, the big income he enjoyed and the professional success that earned him the respect of his peers were clouded by a grueling work schedule and the financial burdens he was carrying.

John's nice home came with a big mortgage. His flashy car came factory-equipped with a sizeable lease payment! His financial planning practice came with long hours of hard work, late nights, and unwanted stress. John was not living the life he wanted to live. He was tired most of the time, financially strapped, and working way too hard for a couple of weeks of vacation a year. Something had to change.

Today, John Burley is the internationally known author of the number one best-selling book *Money Secrets of the Rich*, a sought after financial educator, one of the most successful and innovative investors on two continents, and independently wealthy. Today John enjoys personal and financial freedom. He does what he wants to do when he wants to do it. We'll flesh John's story out more as we move through this book. As we move through his story, we will uncover the eight distinct phases of the change process that you will be able to put to work for yourself as you move toward the life you have always wanted. You will discover that John's change story began where yours will – with the certain belief that a better life must be out there waiting to be lived.

For A FREE Audio Tape
"The 7 Levels of Investor"

Based on the principles taught in
John Burley's #1 International Best Seller
Money Secrets of the Rich!

Call Australia/New Zealand
1300 550 240 or +(61) 2 9662 8488
USA 1-(800) 561 8246
Outside USA 1-(623) 561 8246

That is where Steve Dover's change story began as well. He believed that a better life was out there waiting for him. Steve had been a faithful employee in a large company in Australia for many years. He had worked hard for his employers. He poured out his time and energy on behalf of his company. He was a model employee, consistently outperforming most of his coworkers, and modeling an exemplary work ethic to his peers. Steve made a good living, had most of his weekends off, and was able to maintain a reasonable standard of living. Steve's coworkers and friends thought he had it made. He had a good job, a budding career, and solid job security. However, his contagious smile and keen sense of humor masked his inner dissatisfaction. Something was missing.

From the time Steve was a young boy he dreamed of having more than just enough. Raised by a father who worked hard at a blue-collar job for minimum pay and a mother who spent all of her energy on raising six children, Steve knew what it was like to be plagued by financial worries. So early in his life, Steve decided that he wanted to grow up to be a millionaire businessman. While most young boys dream of being fire fighters, football players, or policemen, Steve dreamed of being a financially successful and self-sufficient entrepreneur. Unlike most young boys who let go of their dreams to become fire fighters, football players, and policemen, Steve never gave up on his dream to become a millionaire businessman.

Steve worked hard for his company, but in the back of his mind he began to realize that his chosen career path was not going to help him fulfill his childhood dream. As he worked hard and brought in clients and accounts for his employers, Steve began to notice that he was making his bosses way more money than he would ever see from them. Steve's company was becoming prosperous as a result of his hard work, but Steve wasn't seeing much of that prosperity. Instead, he was accumulating more and more consumer debt and the mounting pressure that comes from a growing financial burden. Steve wanted to experience a life filled with the prosperity that he knew he was capable of achieving. Rather than spend his years making his employers wealthy, Steve wanted to spend his best years building his own financial future. He knew the life that he dreamed of was out there waiting for him, and he knew that this life was achievable. Steve also knew that his current life path was not going to help him reach his desired goal. Something needed to change.

Today, Steve Dover is a millionaire businessman. He is one of the most inventive and dynamic investors in Australia. He enjoys a life of prosperity and joy as he continues to create solid investments and spends time with the people he loves. He goes surfing several times a week on some of the most beautiful beaches in the world. Beyond that, Steve finds a great deal of satisfaction in building up his companies that are characterized by solid teamwork and a genuine sense of loyalty. Steve even manages to give back to the people of the world by mentoring aspiring investors.

You will read more about Steve Dover and people like him as you move through this book. You will discover that the process that allowed Steve to move away from the position of being a frustrated employee into the exciting territory of achieving his lifelong dreams is a process that you can understand and use to your advantage. Instead of being stuck in a frustrating existence, you can use the power of change to realize the life that you have always wanted to live.

Felicity Heffernan used the power of change to realize her dreams of a better life. Her vision of the life she wanted involved spending more time with her family. Happily married to her husband, Greg, with two beautiful young daughters, Felicity dreamed of the day when she would be able to spend her best waking hours with the people she loved. As it stood, Felicity was spending most of her time pouring out all of her energy on a nine-to-five job. She had a good job as a loan manager for a reputable bank. Her coworkers enjoyed her contagious smile and warm personality. Her bosses valued her loyalty, commitment, and hard work. Professionally speaking, Felicity was in a good place where her abilities were appreciated and her education was being put to good use. The only problem with Felicity's situation was that it didn't look like the life that she would have chosen for herself.

If she could have had her preferences, Felicity would have gotten up every morning, poured out her attention and affection on her husband and her daughters, and lived a life that more accurately reflected her own personal priorities. Instead, like so many others, her mornings looked like the typical working mother sprint to get out of the door and head to the office. Every morning, her alarm clock would go off, and Felicity would spring out of bed, prepare the kids for school, make herself professionally presentable while taking care of her family's needs, and then hop in the car and dash to the office only to arrive completely exhausted and worn out before the day even got started. Felicity wanted to set her own priorities in life, but life was setting her priorities for her. Something had to change.

Today Felicity sets her own priorities. She determines her daily schedule. Instead of being controlled by a time clock, Felicity has the freedom to begin her day at her own pace. She feels better about the job she is doing as a mother, enjoys the quality time she spends with her family, and is at peace with the way she has prioritized her life.

Felicity is still active in the business world, putting what she has learned into practice and living a productive life as she secures a bright financial future for her family. In fact, Felicity owns her own very successful real estate investment company and gains a lot of satisfaction from helping people purchase their own homes. Today, instead of working when a boss tells her she must, Felicity gets to set her own hours to more accurately reflect the priorities she has set for her life.

Something had to change in her life, so Felicity took the necessary steps to make those changes. This book will show you step-by-step what Felicity Heffernan and so many others have done so that you too can move toward experiencing the life you have always wanted to live.

Bryan Fergus woke up one morning with the nagging sense that he wasn't living the life that he had always wanted to live. He was tired all of the time. His typical day began with an early morning and ended with a late night. Most of the time in between was spent handling tedious administrative duties and hurrying to meet one deadline after another. In the meantime, Bryan's three children were growing up while he missed out on their "firsts". Their first steps, their first words, and their first given kisses were events that Bryan's patient wife would report on while he got ready for work in the morning. Instead of witnessing these monumental occasions in the life of his family, Bryan heard about them secondhand, as he got ready to rush out the door.

Beyond missing out on the important moments in the life of his family, Bryan had the terrible feeling that he was also missing out on fulfilling his personal destiny in life. Bryan knew that he had been called to help people find personal peace and joy in life, and yet his own life was seriously lacking both of those vital elements. Instead of enjoying the inner life that he knew was possible, Bryan had allowed an overly hectic schedule to steer him away from inner peace and the fulfillment of his life's purpose. He was respected in his field. He was a sought after speaker, gifted writer and respected educator. However, in his efforts to help everybody else Bryan had overlooked the people that needed his help first and foremost – his family and himself. Something had to change.

Today, Bryan Fergus lives a balanced life. He is devoted husband and father, and is truly moving toward fulfilling his life's purpose. He has restored balance to his days and enjoys the freedom to set his own schedule. He works when he wants to and where he wants to, adjusting his schedule to best serve the needs of his family. Beyond that, Bryan continues to help people find personal peace and joy in life through an active speaking and writing career. Fortunately, today Bryan has learned to pursue his life's purpose with a true sense of peace that comes from living an appropriately balanced life.

The steps that John Burley took toward fulfilling his dream of living a life of personal freedom are the same steps that Steve Dover took toward achieving a life of personal prosperity. The steps that Felicity Heffernan took toward living a life that reflected her true priorities are the same steps that Bryan Fergus took toward living a life that enabled him to fulfill his personal destiny in a balanced way. These people all have one thing in common. They harnessed the power of change and put it to work for themselves to achieve the lives that they always dreamed of living. John, Steve, Felicity, and Bryan were all keenly aware that something needed to change in their lives in order for them to experience life to the fullest. They all took the necessary steps toward making positive changes in their lives, and as a result they began to see their dreams become reality.

Just imagine if you could do that? What if you could harness the power of change and put it to work for you? The good news is that you really can. You can take the necessary steps toward fulfilling your dreams. You can find freedom, experience prosperity, live according to your priorities, fulfill your personal destiny and make whatever changes you feel necessary in your life by putting the information in *Powerful Changes* to work for you.

That is what this book is about. This book isn't simply a collection of inspiring stories about fictitious people who live dream lives. This is a book about the very specific and very real steps that very real people have taken. These steps have empowered them to truly enjoy their days on Planet Earth.

The pages that follow are designed to help you understand the change process and how to put it to work for yourself. Many of the chapters in this book include action steps. We highly recommend that you take advantage of them. These actions steps aren't in this book to simply fill white paper with black ink. These actions steps are designed to help you enter into and proceed with the change process so you can begin to move toward living the life you truly want to live.

Beyond being given the insight and actions steps that will help you proceed with the change process, this book will also identify those beliefs and habits that will help you make the inward adjustments necessary to experience positive change in your life. *Powerful Changes* will also make you aware of the beliefs and habits that hinder some people from making the changes necessary to pursue the lives they want to live. Pay close attention to both the healthy and unhealthy beliefs and actions so you can take full advantage of what we have discovered in the quest to truly understand the power of change.

Change is a powerful force that you can harness and use to your advantage. We have written this book knowing that it will be a valuable tool that will help you make the positive changes that will lead you toward the life you have always dreamed of living. That is why this book was not simply designed to be an inspiring little collection of snapshots of personal successes. We had loftier goals than that when writing *Powerful Changes*.

This book was designed to accomplish three purposes. First, we will explain the change process so you can make *Powerful Changes* for the better in your own life. Second, we will make you aware of the beliefs, systems, and habits that will allow you to experience the *Powerful Changes* that will lead you toward the life you dream of living. Third, we will make you aware of the beliefs and habits that can hinder progress in the change process.

We know from experience that this is the kind of information people want when they pick up a book like this one and begin to read it. People are looking for practical information that will help them experience *Powerful Changes* in life. So, if you plan to read this book in one sitting, then plan to read it twice. Slow down, do the action steps, and get ready to make some amazing and immediate changes for the better in your life.

What qualifies us to write such a book? Well, you have already read part of our stories. We are John Burley and Bryan Fergus. You have already seen that we have both made some fairly substantial personal changes in our lives. Besides our personal experiences with change, we are both educators who have a passion to help people improve their lives in significant ways. We are also close personal friends. Our children have grown up together, we've watched our fair share of science fiction movies together, and tackled too many hot pastrami sandwiches together to count. We've had some amazing conversations over those pastrami sandwiches that have brought us a great deal of understanding and insight into the change process and how it intersects with real life.

Through years of close friendship and personal collaboration we have watched thousands of people make significant life changes and we have come to a greater understanding of the change process and how it works. In this book, we are going to pool our knowledge and personal experiences relating to the subject on change and let you see what we have discovered through the years. You will receive the benefit of the insights drawn from countless conversations and thousands of hours of interviews and research. We are certain that what we have learned through the years will help you harness the power of change and put it to positive use in your life. So read on and begin your change journey. Maybe the best place to start this journey is to invite you to enter into the discovery process with us by telling you about a little experiment we conducted.

Chapter 1

A Whole Lot Of Changing Going On!

Twice every year in the great city of Phoenix, Arizona, USA, John Burley and his powerful team of successful investors and instructors hold two amazing events that have been changing lives for years. They call it the "John Burley Advanced Investing Boot Camp". It's an intensive five-day event during which people learn how to take control of their lives through building a plan to achieve their personal financial freedom. John's Boot Camp has been called "the most comprehensive real estate investing training in the world". That's grand praise, but the reality is that John's Boot Camp is really so much more than that. During the five days of Boot Camp, students are not only given the tools and training they need to succeed in the world of real estate investing, they are also equipped to break through the psychological barriers that keep most people from pursuing personal success and financial freedom. The result is an enormously powerful event that has generated thousands of successful investors.

The consensus opinion is that the Burley Boot Camp is the best available training on the subject in the world. So twice a year students come from all over the planet to the bustling desert city of Phoenix, Arizona to learn how to become advanced investors in the world of real estate. They come from all over the United States, Canada, and Mexico, and from as far away as Australia, New Zealand, South Africa, Asia, Europe and all points in between.

They show up to receive an education that for many has literally changed their lives forever.

John combines a few essential elements that work together to make his training unlike any other. First, John prepares his students for success by sharing his vast knowledge of the principles and practices of profitable investing that he personally gained while building a portfolio of over one thousand investment properties. Students are given the opportunity to learn from John Burley himself. John not only carries around in his head an encyclopedic knowledge of the strategies and techniques that make it possible to successfully invest in real estate, he also shares the benefit of his real world experience as an active investor. John interacts with students in the classroom and in social settings. He also takes his students out into the "street" where they learn firsthand how to actually evaluate properties to determine what is and what isn't a good investment. Students attend real estate auctions on courthouse steps where they learn how to compete in that lucrative niche. He truly gives of himself to insure the success of his students.

The second thing that John does to prepare his students to become financially free investors is exposing them to a team of the brightest and best financial and psychological educators in the world. These trainers share their best material with John's students. Boot Camp students learn all about the available niches in real estate investing as well as techniques that successful investors use to excel in these niches. They also learn about structuring a real estate investing business and taking advantage of the best available tax strategies that will legally allow them to keep the lion's share of their profits. John also goes to great lengths to equip his students for success by bringing in the top expert educators from around the world who help them understand the psychology and beliefs of the world's most successful investors. All in all, the training staff that is assembled for the John Burley Advanced Investing Boot Camp is imminently qualified to equip students to achieve the financial freedom that they truly deserve.

Thirdly, John has also recruited an amazing team of volunteers to coach the Boot Camp students during their training. This staff is made up of volunteers who have all been students themselves at

John's Boot Camp. These graduates have gone on to develop very successful careers as real estate investors. As a result, John has invited them to come back to Boot Camp to assist in coaching new students through their training process. These volunteers come from all over the world and are fully committed to helping others find the financial freedom and personal success that they have achieved as the result of their Boot Camp experience. The standards to qualify to be a Boot camp staff member are very high. Every staff member must be actively investing on a regular basis to be invited to participate in John's Boot Camp.

John's volunteer staff is made up of some of the sharpest and most successful investors in the world. These investors form an extremely diverse group of people. Some are up and coming young men and women who have a passion to squeeze everything they can out of every moment of life. Some are seasoned veterans who have spent years punching a clock and are now looking for a more fulfilling and secure way to prepare for their retirement years. Some of the investors who make up John's Boot camp staff are mothers of young children who have created a source of passive income that has allowed them to invest from their homes while their children are young. Others are couples that would rather spend their time working together than being separated by different careers. Some of the Boot Camp staffers have been victims of corporate downsizing, while others consciously chose to walk away from high paying jobs in the palaces of the corporate world in order to pursue their dreams and control their own destinies. Without a doubt, John's team of volunteer staff members form a cohesive group of diverse people who are passionate about helping others take control of their lives by pursuing their financial freedom. These staff members have all successfully made *Powerful Changes* that have positively transformed their lives. For that reason, John decided that their stories were worth examining.

In April of 2002, John decided to capture the stories of these volunteer staff members. He was hoping that collecting their stories and publishing them in a book might provide the inspiration that some people need to move toward their own personal freedom and financial abundance. John called on his good friend, Bryan Fergus, to conduct a series of intensive interviews designed to get beyond the simple numbers of real estate transactions and the mere statistics of success to determine what really made this remarkable collection of financially savvy people so successful. John knew that Bryan's experience as a spiritual director, accomplished educator, and student of human behavior would allow him to uncover the emotions and beliefs that allowed these staff members to move beyond a life of settling and mediocrity to the pursuit and achievement of their personal goals and dreams.

Bryan spent individual time with every volunteer member of John's Boot Camp staff. He asked probing questions that were designed to explore the emotions and inner thoughts that these successful investors experienced as they took their first steps toward personal financial freedom through real estate investing. Over the course of several Burley Boot Camps, Bryan conducted a large number of interviews. He was instantly impressed by two facts that became very apparent after the first few interviews – the diversity of the people who had experienced *Powerful Changes* in their lives and the similarity of the paths they had walked in the pursuit of those changes.

Bryan was genuinely amazed by the diversity of the types of people who had found success and meaning by making the necessary changes to insure their financial freedom and fulfillment in life. Bryan quickly discovered that the staff members who have achieved their personal financial freedom through implementing the strategies that they learned at John Burley's Advanced Investing Boot Camp are in many ways as different as night and day. This discovery blew away some commonly held false beliefs about the types of people who are able to get ahead in life.

These false beliefs or misconceptions are commonly held and widely crippling in their power to keep many people from realizing their full potential in life. For instance, there is a common misconception floating around in the minds of many people that leads them to believe that only a certain kind of person can achieve personal fulfillment and financial success in life. Many people believe that in order to truly make it "big" in life, a person has to be cut from a certain type of cloth. This stereotypical misconception asserts that only people who come from positions of privilege are really able to get ahead. Putting it simply, this false belief claims that if a person has received a unique and rare privilege like being blessed with a comprehensive education from an Ivy League school, only then will that person be able to get ahead financially. Along these same lines of reasoning, some believe that if a person has been raised in affluence by parents who have been financially successful and truly self-actualized, only then will he or she be able to get ahead financially. The misconception that only the privileged get ahead was dashed to pieces by the diversity of John's Boot Camp staff members.

The same thing happened to the false belief that claims that only the lucky get ahead in life. Some people cling to the misconception that that only people who stumble upon one lucky break after another are able to live the life that most people only dream about. These confused people hold the false notion that success is a matter of luck and nothing more. As a result, many people spend their lives waiting for their lucky break while they settle for mediocrity and misery.

Need proof of the existence of this misconception? State lotteries verify that hundreds of thousands of people in America buy into this misconception on a regular basis. Statisticians tell us that the odds of winning a large lottery jackpot are hopelessly out of reach for most people. In fact, a person has a greater chance of being struck by lightning while being trampled by a herd of circus elephants than he does of winning a multi-million dollar lottery prize. But still, every year thousands of Americans who predominantly fall into the lower one third of household income levels, take their hard earned dollars and use them to buy lottery tickets. These people have bought into the misconception that a turn of impossibly good luck is their only chance of making it in life.

Unfortunately, the negative sides of these misconceptions also hold back the people who buy into them. For instance, the people who buy into the idea that only the privileged get ahead often look at their lack of privilege and give up the hope of even trying to realize their dreams in life. These people hopelessly assume that because they lack an Ivy League education or the benefit of a wealthy upbringing, they are forever doomed to flounder in life. In the minds of these "victims", they either lack the education, mentoring or head start in life that they believe enable successful people to shine.

To be sure, there are some places on this planet where getting ahead financially is difficult indeed. In some third world countries run by maniacal dictators, quite often the only people who are able to flourish in life are those born into positions of privilege. In some societies, caste systems and racial prejudices keep many people from being able to move toward a fully abundant life. However, the misconception that in the "free" or "western" world, the people who have gotten ahead have done so exclusively because of some privileged status granted at birth just doesn't stand up to scrutiny.

The truth is that people from all walks of life have been able to thrive in the free world. Some of the most successful people in the world's history started out with several strikes against them. Some of America's most prominent and respected presidents were raised in abject poverty. Some of the world's most celebrated entertainers come from destitute neighborhoods where people are more concerned with how to survive from one day to the next than they are with how to plan for their retirement or strategize their personal financial freedom. Some of the most distinguished business executives and industrialists in history had to pull themselves up out of dire living conditions and make some significant personal changes before they found success and prosperity. People of privilege are not the only ones who get ahead, and people without a privileged heritage aren't hopelessly doomed to lives of mediocrity. People from all backgrounds and socioeconomic situations are able to thrive by putting the power of change to work for themselves.

The truth is that many of the misconceptions that exist today about the types of people who are able to get ahead and succeed in life simply aren't true. In fact, in many cases many of these misconceptions are nothing more than excuses made by people who aren't willing to take responsibility for the direction of their lives. It is true that unfortunate circumstances can keep some people from moving toward the achievement of their life dreams. Being born with a mental illness or struggling with serious emotional problems can cripple a life if not handled appropriately. As noted above, being born in a country ruled by a mad dictator or being oppressed by a caste system can present severe obstacles to the pursuit of a dream. These facts clearly need to be recognized. At the same time, however, many people who don't get ahead financially in life or move toward fulfilling their life-long dreams are held back because they make choices on a daily basis that take them in the opposite direction.

For example, instead of setting aside money for retirement or placing ten percent of their income in an investment plan each month as John Burley advocates in his best-selling book *Money Secrets of the Rich*, many people go out and rack up huge consumer debts on things that they will be selling at garage sales long before they are ever paid off! When many of these people look at their paycheck-to-paycheck lives, they blame their financial situations on the fact that they weren't born into a wealthy family. In reality, they held the shovel that dug the financial hole in which they are living.

Some people fall into the same unhealthy pattern of blame when it comes to their choice of career. Maybe someone spent his young adult years dreaming of becoming an architect or social worker, but instead chose to spend his entire life trapped in a low-paying eight-to-five job. Let's say that person never made a serious attempt to enroll in a single college course that would move him in the direction he desired. Rather than pursue his dream of designing elaborate buildings or helping people in distress find relief, his dream stayed locked away in his mind and never saw the light of day.

That person could blame fate for the direction his life took, but unfortunately the fact of the matter is that at some level he is making a choice to stay in an unhappy and miserable situation. Or take the overweight person who dreams of being in good physical condition. If that person chooses to go through life blaming genetics without ever trying to control food intake or exercise regularly, who is to blame – fate or a lack of self control?

Obviously, generalizations are being made here, but the point still remains valid. Many people who get ahead in life are not unfairly blessed by being handed easy opportunities or being born into privilege. Many of the people who have gotten ahead financially or fulfilled their lifelong dreams have done so as the result of a lot of hard work and gut determination. At the same time, many people who haven't excelled financially or pursued their dreams have done so in part as the result of their own choices. In fact, when it comes to tapping into the power of change and putting it to work for yourself in a positive way, a lot of it boils down to simply making decisions that are in your best interests and consistently acting on them. More on that later. The truth is that average people from all walks of life are capable of achieving their goals and living their dreams.

As Bryan interviewed John Burley's Boot Camp staff members, he quickly discovered that the keys to personal success and positive change had nothing to do with a certain type of personality or a certain amount of privilege in life. He also found that luck certainly had little to do with a person's ability to get ahead in this world. These people, who had found fulfillment and freedom in life, had done so with little regard to their personal station or starting point in life. Privilege and luck had nothing to do with the success they enjoyed. They weren't all from a special breed of people blessed with higher IQ's than most. They weren't all graduates from prestigious colleges. They weren't all exceptionally talented or particularly gifted in a certain area of life. John's Boot Camp staff members come from a variety of walks of life with vastly different backgrounds.

As we mentioned earlier, the Boot Camp staff members are in many ways as different as night and day. Some are graduates of prominent business schools, but some never even graduated from high school. Some were raised in financially affluent homes by parents who were doctors or high level business executives while some were raised in homes by single mothers who were barely able to pay the bills or blue-collar fathers who made an average wage for hard manual labor. Some of the Boot Camp staff members were raised by short-order cooks and construction workers, while others were raised by restaurant owners and land developers. The diversity that John's Boot Camp staff members represent is amazing. Men and women from all walks of life have been able to find success and meaning by making the necessary changes to insure their financial freedom and fulfillment in life. Again, their personalities and positions in life were as different as night and day.

However, the paths that these people walked on their journeys toward the changed lives they longed to live were remarkably similar. In fact, they were virtually identical. After a handful of interviews with John's Boot Camp staff members, Bryan realized that he was hearing the same story over and over again. The details were obviously different, but the broad pen strokes of the stories unfolding before him were basically the same.

The successful people who agreed to be interviewed all began their stories by telling Bryan how unfulfilled they had been in their former careers or lifestyles. Many complained of not having enough time to spend with their husbands or wives because their previous jobs demanded so much of their focused time and energy. Others talked about being on the road all of the time, traveling from city to city or continent to continent for companies that underpaid and overworked them. Some talked about the birth stories of their young children and how the thought of being away from them in order to pour out their energy and strength on jobs that they literally hated had led them to totally reassess the direction of their lives. It became very apparent that the change stories that led John Burley's Boot Camp staff members to radically change their lives all began with a certain degree of dissatisfaction or feelings of living what to them were unfulfilled lives.

The stories of these staff members would then turn toward an intense Trigger Event that served as the final catalyst that propelled them to make *Powerful Changes* in the way they were living their lives. The catalysts that the Boot Camp staff members talked about ranged from anything as positive as the birth of a child, a wedding or even hearing an inspirational story to the death of a spouse, a terrible auto accident, or being fired from a life-long and loved career. These catalytic events thrust these diverse people into a place where they knew they needed to make some changes if they were ever going to be able to live their dreams. Beyond that, these Trigger Events were so captivating that these staff members knew they would never again be content with the status quo of their previously average lives. After experiencing a Trigger Event of the magnitude that moved them toward dramatic changes in their lives, the thought of going back to their former lives was more painful than the thought of moving forward into uncharted territory.

The stories heard from this collection of now successful investors and willing volunteers would often turn toward the description of a period of searching for a solution to their uncomfortable situations. Once the powerful catalyst of a Trigger Event had driven these people out of their comfort zones, they then went on a Search to find a course of action that would empower them to pursue their dreams and fulfill their visions of the way they wanted their lives to unfold. Some went back to school to train for a second career. Some attended a seminar, read a stack of books, or spent some time traveling and visiting with friends in search of some greater insight for living. Some went on exhaustive internet searches, talked to successful relatives, or spent a great deal of time in prayer in an effort to find a path that would lead to their success and fulfillment in life.

After describing a period of searching, John's Boot Camp staff members would then describe a remarkable discovery that became the solution to their Search for a fulfilling life path. This Discovery of a Door that shed further light on their journey toward personal fulfillment and in many cases financial freedom often took the form of a book they read or a seminar they attended. This Discovery of a Door took many other forms as well. For many of John's Boot camp staffers, the door they discovered was attending his Automatic Wealth Seminar, Advanced Investing Boot Camp or one of the other seminars that John conducts where they learned how to strategize their financial freedom so they could be freed up to pursue their lifelong dreams.

At the same time, some of the discovery stories that Bryan heard described subtle discoveries that led to more opportunities down the path. For instance, for some of the successful investors that Bryan interviewed, their discovery stories centered on the chance meeting of a new friend who served as a sounding board. In many cases this new relationship brought greater clarity and even made the staff member aware of greater possibilities.

An interesting fact to note about this step toward *Powerful Changes* was the transformation of emotion that occurred at this point in the process. The Dissatisfaction, unhappiness, or lack of fulfillment in life that compelled these people to Search for a better way to live was often replaced by relief during this step in the change process. In fact, each phase of this process seemed to be characterized by its own distinct emotion. This idea will be explored in depth a little later in this book.

Discovery then propelled these people toward action. As Bryan listened to story after story it became obvious that Taking Action was a very important step or phase in the change process that these people underwent in pursuit of a better life. Dissatisfaction, Trigger Events, Searches and discoveries all led to some decisive action that needed to be taken. This became the definitive step – the "crossroads" experience – that forced people to either "put up or shut up" when it came to the pursuit of their dreams.

The Boot Camp staff members described different kinds of action steps. These were as varied as the different personalities of the people Bryan interviewed. In the context of interviewing John's staff members, the first action step taken usually centered around doing their first real estate deal. For some it involved quitting their jobs, which forced them to Take Action, and made it impossible to turn back in the change process. Taking Action became a dramatic step on the path to change that truly cemented the decision to change in the minds and hearts of John's staff members. Taking Action also became a remarkably empowering experience for these people. By Taking Action they proved to themselves and the people closest to them that they were serious about living the lives of their dreams.

After Taking Action, the Boot Camp staff members discovered that the change process also involved a period of Refining their action plan. Once action was taken and the process of change had cleared that important hurdle, these successful investors often discovered that slight adjustments needed to be made if they were going to reach their life goals. For instance, one staff member described how his investing strategy needed to be adjusted to take into account changes in the national economy. Another described how the speed of his action plan needed to be slowed down a little bit in order for his wife to feel comfortable and supportive of the new path they were walking together in life. Action usually led to adjustment. Both were critically important to insure success.

The next phase of the *Powerful Changes* Process involved Perseverance. Bryan heard story after story of how John's Boot Camp staff members had to believe in their change strategies long enough for "lag" to allow them to work. Simply Discovering a Door to a better life and then Taking Action to walk through that door was not enough to guarantee the success of their strategies. These people had been given enough insight into what it would take to get ahead financially to realize that they had to give their strategies time to work.

John Burley himself had given them this insight during their experience as Boot Camp students. John has been investing in real estate long enough to realize that one of the key components in investing success is lag. Lag is the simple principle best illustrated by the biblical statement, "You reap what you sow." These students had been trained by John Burley to give their investing strategies enough time to go to work for them.

Bryan discovered while talking to John's staff members that this lag principle translated into Perseverance as they walked down the path to the better life they were working toward. In other words, as these people implemented their strategies, they went through a phase in the change process that required them to stick to those strategies and plans without altering them too drastically. They understood that if they veered too far off the path, they would so fundamentally alter their course of action that they would never discover if their strategy would truly work. "Sticking to it" is a key element in the process that allowed these people to achieve their dreams and find meaning and fulfillment in their lives.

One of the defining elements that characterized the stories that Bryan heard involved the commitment of these remarkable people to continued personal and professional growth. After experiencing a major change, John's Boot Camp staff members came to the realization that life in itself is a series of changes that can be either tolerated or capitalized upon. John's staff members enjoyed a comfortable amount of success, freedom and fulfillment in life, but they also understood the importance of being open to change in all areas of their lives as they continued to grow and thrive. The change process that these people had worked through had so completely altered who they were that they now viewed themselves as people empowered to harness the power of change for their benefit in every area of their lives. In fact, many of these people were so committed to Continued Growth that they established accountability relationships with others who would spur them on to even further growth. This combination of a commitment to Continued Growth coupled with rigorous accountability served to move these people toward even greater progress than they had ever imagined.

After conducting interviews for over eighteen months, Bryan reviewed all of the stories that he had heard. As he compared notes from different interviews, eight common phases or steps in the *Powerful Changes* Process began to emerge. Over the course of this time, Bryan was given the opportunity to interview other highly successful people. Some were John's Boot Camp staffers, others were up and coming investors, and others were successful in other arenas of life. Bryan interviewed some people who had simply transformed tough circumstances and true adversity into opportunities to take control of their lives and pursue their dreams. Through all of these interviews, Bryan saw these common steps taken toward *Powerful Changes* emerge time and time again. Without leaving out one step or skipping one phase, each person who had made significant changes that led to a more fulfilling and enjoyable life had worked through each of the eight phases of the *Powerful Changes* Process that we have been discussing in this chapter.

The people who had found success and fulfillment in life were as different as night and day. However, the process they had moved through toward the total transformation of their lives all followed an eight-stepped path. Those steps or phases in the *Powerful Changes* Process are:

- **Step 1 – Dissatisfaction**
- **Step 2 – Trigger Event**
- **Step 3 – The Search**
- **Step 4 – Discovering the Door**
- **Step 5 – Taking Action**
- **Step 6 – Refining**
- **Step 7 – Persistence**
- **Step 8 – Continued Growth**

Without fail, every person who Bryan interviewed had passed through each of these phases as they moved toward the lives they dreamed of living. Of course, this wasn't a process that any of them were consciously working through at the time. They made their way from one step of the *Powerful Changes* Process to the next without really understanding where their inner thoughts and emotions were carrying them. Only after they had reached Step 7, the Persistence phase, were they able to look back and see the path their lives had taken.

It is said that hindsight is always 20/20. What if you could benefit from the hindsight and insight that these successful people gained as they looked back over the change experiences that they went through? What if you could use that hindsight and insight to help yourself move along that path? What if, rather than stumbling along in the dark as you look for a path that will help you find the peace, fulfillment and freedom you're after, you could follow a clearly marked path that has been traveled by many before you? And what if the testimony of those who had already traveled this road assured you that it did indeed lead to *Powerful Changes*, positive growth and better life? Would you be willing to take a closer look at the way marked out before you?

Chances are pretty good that since you are reading this book, you are probably interested in taking some positive growth steps in your life. You are probably interested in understanding the process that leads to *Powerful Changes* in greater depth. You are probably even trying to determine where you are in that process yourself as you pursue your dreams and personal goals.

The next several chapters of this book will give you a closer look at the different phases of the *Powerful Changes* Process. Each phase will be clearly defined. You will read real life stories that describe what these phases looked like to others who have already moved through them. These stories won't be prescriptive; they will be descriptive. In other words, your story doesn't have to look exactly like these stories of others who have gone before you on this path to a better life. These change "snapshots" will simply serve to take some abstract concepts and make them more concrete. As each phase is explored, you will also gain an understanding of the underlying emotion that characterizes each phase. This "feeling barometer" will help you get a handle on the emotional process that people go through as they move through a major life change. In addition, looking at these emotions will help you determine where you are in the process of making the changes that will bring you closer to living your ideal life.

After exploring each phase, you will be encouraged to take a few simple actions steps. These steps aren't designed to rush you through the change process. However, having a clear understanding of the steps of the *Powerful Changes* Process will save you some time in the long run. Understanding the different phases of growth that have allowed successful people to achieve their success and fulfillment will help you move along a sure path to your ideal life without being sidetracked. Our desire is that by becoming familiar with the *Powerful Changes* Process you will be able to put the power of change to work for yourself. With that said, let's turn our attention to the starting point in the *Powerful Changes* Process: Dissatisfaction.

For a FREE 25 Page Report on

"The Seven Levels of Investor"

Visit www.johnburley.com.

Chapter 2

Dissatisfied With Settling

Dissatisfaction Defined

Nobody likes the cold, wintry feelings that accompany Dissatisfaction. Restlessness, unhappiness, and helplessness are the demons that plague a person living through a season of personal dissatisfaction with life. Dissatisfaction is the constant companion of the person who knows that things could be better, but simply aren't. In extreme cases hopelessness can flood a heart and paralyze a life that has lived in a state of Dissatisfaction for too long. Dissatisfaction drives some people to take desperate action in the hope that somehow their knee jerk responses will make the pain of their personal unhappiness go away and stay away.

What is dissatisfaction? We all know what dissatisfaction is from an experiential point of view, because we have all felt it to some degree at one time or another. We've all experienced that nagging feeling that tells us that life should be better than it is. That's dissatisfaction. Sometimes dissatisfaction feels like a restlessness in our souls that just won't go away. Sometimes dissatisfaction feels like an annoying sense of boredom that keeps us from enjoying any given moment. Put simply, dissatisfaction is a strong inner sense of unhappiness and restlessness. Or to put it another way, dissatisfaction is a gripping desire to improve an unacceptable situation. When we are no longer satisfied with the status quo, we are *dissatisfied*. When we are certain that life could be better than it is, we are *dissatisfied*. Dissatisfaction is a strong inner urge to change things from the way they are to the way they could be. For that very reason, dissatisfaction is a powerful motivator for change.

It was dissatisfaction that led the early colonial patriots of America to rebel against the steep taxes levied against them by the King of England. In desperation, men like George Washington, Thomas Jefferson, and Benjamin Franklin launched a revolution against seemingly impossible odds. Their desperate actions, spurred on by a tremendous and overpowering sense of injustice and dissatisfaction, led to the establishment of one of the greatest countries that has ever existed on this planet. Dissatisfaction drove these men to act to alleviate their pain. As a result, they became the fathers of a great nation.

An inner sense of dissatisfaction can motivate people to move out of their discomfort zones and pursue their dreams. Often dissatisfaction can drive people to do some very courageous and ultimately good things. A certain amount of dissatisfaction drove Orville and Wilbur Wright to become the pioneers of aviation. If they had been content with traveling by train or horse or even automobile, they never would have endured the hard work and walked the tough road of discovery and invention. Thankfully they pushed ahead and were among the first to leave the ground in their primitive airplane.

Imagine the courage and determination these men must have had as they climbed into their airplanes time after time to take a test flight. Defying gravity is a courageous thing, and these men were among the first to try it behind the steering sticks of an airplane. That's real courage. At the same time we need to remember that this real courage was fueled by some very real dissatisfaction. Today, we are able to travel around the world at incredible speeds in large part due to the dissatisfaction and discontentment that drove these men to excel. The inner dissatisfaction of the Wright brothers was the starting point that led to an innovation in travel that has changed life on Planet Earth forever.

Dissatisfaction does drive people to do some great and courageous things, but if someone stays too dissatisfied and discontent for too long they can be driven to do some things that are not so good. Frustration and dissatisfaction over extreme poverty, injustice, and social neglect causes thousands of

American teenagers to get involved in urban gangs every year. Dissatisfaction over the way things are and the belief that life will never allow them to rise above their surroundings can quickly transform a young life full of promise and opportunity into a life filled with utter despair. In many cases, despair turns to anger, and anger gets channeled into unhealthy and even criminal behavior.

Dissatisfaction Is A Warning Sign

The bottom line of all of this is that Dissatisfaction needs to be taken seriously. Dissatisfaction can drive people to do great things and it can drive others into despair, but it never drives a person to do nothing. Dissatisfaction never urges a person who is discontented and unhappy with an unacceptable situation to simply sit still.

Dissatisfaction can be ignored for a while. When the heart fills with dissatisfaction and discontentment we can fill the head with entertainment. We can even turn up the volume in our lives to drown out the messages that dissatisfaction whispers to us. We can pick up the pace of our schedules and try to battle Dissatisfaction by keeping busy, but if we do we will just wear ourselves out. Try as we might, in the quiet moments of life, Dissatisfaction will sneak back into our consciousness and rear its ugly head. It will remind us that we are stuck in an unacceptable situation.

When the alarm clock goes off and we climb out of bed in the morning, Dissatisfaction will remind us that our lives are going to be the same today as they were yesterday if we don't listen to the unhappiness and discontentment inside of us brought on by Dissatisfaction. When we lay our heads down on our pillows and are forced to listen to the thoughts in our heads for a moment, if we are stuck in a state of Dissatisfaction it can dominate our thoughts and even keep us awake at night.

Dissatisfaction needs to be taken seriously, because dissatisfaction is a warning sign. Dissatisfaction is the yellow flashing barricade light on the freeway of our lives that warns us that if we keep going in the same direction, we are headed for despair.

The truth is that the human mind is an amazing thing. It continually processes all of the thoughts, attitudes, emotions, and experiences that the world throws at us on a daily basis. All of these elements are stored in our minds on an either conscious or subconscious level. All of these factors – our thoughts, attitudes, emotions, and experiences – have a deep impact on us. These factors shape and mold us into the people we are, and when something enters our psyche that doesn't quite fit with the way we imagine our lives should be, Dissatisfaction starts to set in.

Maybe all of the lessons that we were taught when we were children by our parents and teachers communicated to us that we are truly special people with great destinies before us. If our lives don't look all that great, the inner discord that occurs when these early thoughts of greatness and our outer circumstances of mediocrity collide can cause a great deal of dissatisfaction. In a situation like this, we will walk around with the nagging sense that things are supposed to be different than they are. The distance between the way things could be and the way things are causes dissatisfaction to set in. This feeling of being dissatisfied then plagues every moment of our lives with a variety of emotions that we will discuss in the next few pages. Dissatisfaction is a warning sign. It needs to be taken seriously, and not simply ignored or pushed out of our minds by filling our heads with entertainment or noise.

Dissatisfaction Is The Beginning of Change

Beyond being a warning sign, Dissatisfaction is the beginning of change. Here's how that works: Our amazing minds warn us that things aren't the way we really want them to be. Then our minds make us so uncomfortable with an overpowering inner sense of dissatisfaction, unhappiness, and discontentment that we are prompted and even forced to do something to make the pain go away. Look at this sense of dissatisfaction as a built-in motivator that keeps us from becoming stagnant in life. If channeled in the right direction, Dissatisfaction can move us toward fulfilling our dreams of a better life.

As Bryan interviewed John Burley's Boot Camp staff members, it became clear that every single one of them began their journey on the path to significant and lasting change by realizing that they were dissatisfied to some degree with their lives. Dissatisfaction was the catalyst that caused them to move in the direction of improving their lives. Simply put, Dissatisfaction was the first chapter of their Powerful Change stories.

All of John's Boot Camp staff members are successful real estate investors. As Bryan interviewed them, he asked each of them this simple question: Why did you choose to become a real estate investor? Invariably, John's Boot Camp staffers answered this question by telling a story about an inner sense of dissatisfaction over the way they were living their lives. This Dissatisfaction pushed them to make some amazing changes. Let's look at a few of their stories.

Adrian Oakman's Story

Adrian Oakman's story of Dissatisfaction gives us a good snapshot of what this first phase in the Powerful Changes Process is really all about. If you were to meet Adrian today, you would be impressed by his infectious smile and love for life. Adrian walks around with a true sense of gratitude for the life that he enjoys. Today, Adrian is a successful real estate investor in New Zealand. In fact, he is the premiere real estate investor using the "cash flow" niche to create steady and abundant positive cash flow for himself, his family and his investors.

Cash flow, or the wrap niche (as some refer to it), in real estate investing is simple enough to understand. Some people try to make it complex, but in reality, wrapping a property is nothing more than using a simple financing vehicle to remarket a property for the purpose of creating passive income. In a real estate wrap, an investor acquires a property at a wholesale price. He then finds an occupant who takes possession of the property from him. The investor carries the financing for the new occupant. The buyer pays the investor a new higher monthly payment than the mortgage the investor took out on the property. The investor pays the original mortgage payments and keeps the difference or "the spread" as it is called. The investor makes money by keeping the spread. At the same time, since the occupant is working toward owning the property and not just renting, the investor doesn't have to be a landlord. He is spared from all of the late night repair calls. He doesn't have to spend his time unclogging toilets or fixing broken windows. All the cash flow investor has to do is collect the money. There are different variations on the cash flow niche theme, but they all essentially boil down to this simple and basic concept.

John Burley is one of the premiere cash flow investors in America. He has pioneered wrap strategies in several states and has taught thousands of people in a number of different countries how to use this strategy to discover their own personal financial freedom. Adrian learned this simple strategy from John and has put it to remarkable use in New Zealand. Today, Adrian enjoys a healthy passive income that allows him to spend his time doing the things he wants to do. However, it wasn't always this way for Adrian.

Before Adrian made a positive change and became the successful real estate investor that he is today, he was a dairy farmer in a small town outside of Wellington, New Zealand. Dairy farming is hard work. Adrian would get up well before dawn every morning to get started with his day. He would spend his day doing backbreaking labor that involved everything from milking and feeding dairy cows to the dozens of chores that have to be done to keep a working farm in truly working order.

Adrian experienced early mornings and late nights seven days a week, 365 days a year. Dairy cows have to be milked on a tight schedule or they stop producing. If the cows stop producing, there is no milk to sell. If there is no milk to sell, there is no way for a dairy farmer to make a living and provide for his family. The lot of a dairy farmer in life is hard work, exhausting days, and constant pressure.

As if the hard work wasn't enough, Adrian had to deal with the market fluctuations that trouble most farming industries. If production is down or if the cost of feed rises or if the price of his product drops, any farmer is forced to make financial sacrifices that bring their own set of burdens. Many people have the luxury of a constant paycheck that they can depend upon coming on the same two days every month. Most people know that their paychecks will be for a set amount of money that they can count on. Farmers don't enjoy that kind of certainty. So many different factors can enter the mix and change a farmer's income from one month to the next. The result is a constant financial pressure that creates a tremendous amount of stress for a farming family. This financial pressure coupled with all of the hard work that he had to perform every single day of every single year began to have a negative impact on Adrian's zest for life.

Beyond his demanding work, Adrian also had a family that needed his attention. Adrian's wife needed a husband, and Adrian's children needed their father. Adrian's family is the joy of his life. Adrian wanted to be around his family more. He has two beautiful children and a wife named Tracey who lights up a room when she walks into it. Adrian wanted to spend his time with his loving family rather than with a herd of dairy cows.

Adrian was wise enough to understand that being a husband and a father brings its own set of responsibilities. Children need their father to guide and direct them in life. A wife needs the help of her husband when it comes to managing a household. If a marriage is to stay alive and thriving, it requires a certain amount of quality time from both people involved. Adrian knew all of these things to be true, and yet he was stuck in a tough job that demanded more from him than he wanted to give. Adrian got tired of sacrificing his family time on the altar of dairy farming.

Adrian hung in there for a long time. The belief in words like honor and integrity are very important to him. Adrian's work ethic is amazing. In spite of his physical fatigue and his inner sense of discontentment, Adrian always gave his best effort. However, being constantly pulled away from the family that he desired to be with to a demanding job that was taking its toll on his family life started to get old. That inner pull from his family to his job was the warning sign of Dissatisfaction telling Adrian that something needed to change. Things could not stay the same. For Adrian the situation had become unacceptable. He simply could not imagine living this way for the rest of his life. As mentioned above, Adrian did make some Powerful Changes. Today he is a very successful real estate investor who now has the luxury of setting his own schedule. Adrian is truly happy today. For quite a while Adrian struggled with strong feelings of Dissatisfaction. The starting point of Adrian's journey toward satisfaction and success was coming to terms with the fact that he was dissatisfied to the point of discontentment.

Lasting change begins by coming to terms with Dissatisfaction. Rather than masking it or ignoring it, Dissatisfaction needs to be recognized for what it is. Instead of pretending that feelings of dissatisfaction are nothing more than unbridled restlessness, we need to realize that Dissatisfaction is a warning sign that discontentment and despair are real possibilities if changes aren't made. We need to realize that Dissatisfaction is the first phase in the Powerful Changes Process. Dissatisfaction can be the first step toward positive change if we take it seriously and allow it to propel us in the right direction. Adrian understood that and took the necessary steps to make the positive changes that have enabled him to live the life he has always dreamed of living.

We will get back to Adrian's story in an upcoming chapter. The journey he took toward the fulfillment of his dreams is truly inspiring and definitely worth looking at in further detail in order to better understand the Powerful Changes Process. Adrian's story has inspired hundreds of people to move beyond their Dissatisfaction to pursue their personal dreams of success and happiness.

Joe Arlt's Story

Adrian's change story is one of many change stories that begin with recognizing Dissatisfaction for what it is. Dissatisfaction is the first step or phase in the Powerful Changes Process. It's the warning sign that tells us that something has to change or we will never experience true joy and fulfillment in life.

Joe Arlt's change journey also began with a strong sense of being dissatisfied with his life. Joe's situation in life was simply unacceptable to him, even though many people would have envied his life. Dissatisfaction is often subtle that way. Often the people experiencing Dissatisfaction are the only ones who know that it is present in their lives. This was the case for Joe. Most people were not able to tell that Joe was truly dissatisfied with the direction his life was taking. In fact, most people would have coveted Joe's life.

Joe was born and raised on the east coast of the United States. He grew up and went away to a good college. After getting his bachelor's degree, Joe pressed on and got his Master of Business Administration degree from Wharton, one of the most prestigious business schools in the world. Armed with a great education, a winning personality, and a strong desire to climb the corporate ladder, Joe landed a prestigious corporate job that allowed him to travel.

As Joe traveled the world representing his company, he began to excel in his field. Joe was a corporate whiz. His bosses appreciated his hard work and determination. His passion for excellence and his desire to make a mark in the business world made Joe a valuable employee. He was respected by his peers and appreciated by his bosses. To the outside observer, it looked as though Joe had it made. He was living the life that business school students dream of. He had the kind of job that many people fantasize about. His job was exactly the kind of job that young corporate wannabe's fight tooth and nail to get. On top of all of that, Joe got to experience the glamorous world of corporate travel. Some people dream of traveling the world. Joe's bosses paid him to do just that. In the eyes of many people, Joe had it made.

The only problem was that Joe just wasn't all that happy. He quickly discovered that the glamorous world of corporate travel isn't really all that glamorous. Early morning races through rush hour traffic to catch a plane got old fast. "Red eye" flights, lousy airline food, and being away from family and friends added up to ridiculous stress levels. The pressure to perform in the corporate world and the constant threat of being "outdone" by someone else began to weigh heavily upon Joe.

Beyond all of that, Joe discovered that when it all came down to it, he didn't really fit into the corporate mold. Joe is an entrepreneur. Entrepreneurs are happiest and at their best when they are using their intellect and abilities to create systems of wealth. Joe was working someone else's system. He was traipsing all over the world in an effort to make a corporate conglomerate successful. Joe wanted to make his own mark in the world in his own way. He truly wanted to be the captain of his own ship.

This difference between what Joe wanted out of life and what his position in life actually was caused him to experience a tremendous amount of dissatisfaction. He wanted to be his own boss and use his creativity and intellect to achieve great things. Instead, he was spending his best time and using his best energy on promoting someone else's product.

This disagreement between the life Joe wanted and the life Joe had was compounded by the fact that his current career path was in many ways the fulfillment of an earlier dream. Sometimes people are faced with the strange dilemma of fulfilling their dreams only to realize that what they thought would bring personal fulfillment to their lives really doesn't. Celebrities often face this predicament. After desiring fame and working hard to get it, celebrities often discover that the price of fame is higher than the price they want to pay. The lack of privacy and constant scrutiny become difficult to tolerate. Harsh words by fickle critics become disheartening. The desire for fame becomes replaced by a desire for obscurity. That happens sometimes with dreams. Some people start out in life knowing what they want, but they don't always experience fulfillment and joy when they get what they were after!
Joe struggled with this. He had the dream job of most young, budding corporate executives. He thought that the challenge of successfully rising to the top of the corporate heap would give him a sense of purpose and meaning in life. He was hoping for more control of his time and more direction of his energy. At the end of the day, he had neither. Joe was dissatisfied. His inner life was plagued by a strong sense of dissatisfaction and unhappiness. He was compelled to make some changes to improve his unacceptable situation. Something had to change. Today Joe is a successful entrepreneur. He has used his intellect and creativity to develop his own system of wealth. He enjoys the freedom to do what he wants to do when he wants to do it. At the same time, Joe has found new meaning and fulfillment in life by being actively involved in charities all over the world. Joe's success in business has empowered him along

with his wife, Karen, to become a generous financial supporter of charitable efforts that benefit the human community. His old dream of climbing the corporate ladder has been replaced by the new dream of being able to help alleviate some of the pain and suffering throughout the world. He is putting his keen intellect and creative mind to use in order to benefit humanity. Most importantly, Joe is happy. Joe's journey toward happiness began with Dissatisfaction. This Dissatisfaction prompted him to make some Powerful Changes that ultimately led to a better life. Even though it is incredibly uncomfortable, Dissatisfaction seems to be a necessary element in the process of change. It's a step that every person intent on making Powerful Changes has to go through.

Felicity Heffernan's Story

You've already met Felicity Heffernan. Felicity was the working mother mentioned in the introduction to this book. You've already heard a piece of her story, but it's worth looking at briefly again, simply because Dissatisfaction played such a powerful role in her journey toward a better life for herself and her family.

Only working mothers can understand the tension between needing and even wanting to work and at the same time wanting to be with their children. Of course, working fathers want to be with their children as well, but the bond between a mother and child is a truly powerful force. That's probably one of the reasons why many working mothers struggle so much with Dissatisfaction when it comes to reconciling their professional careers with their roles as mothers. This was the tension that Felicity dealt with on a daily basis. Every morning as she struggled to meet the demands of getting her family ready to meet the day and getting herself to work, she also struggled with wanting to have more time to be the mother she truly wanted to be.

As we saw in the introduction to this book, Felicity had a good job. She was a respected loan manager at a good bank. She had the appreciation and admiration of her coworkers and her employers. Felicity was the kind of employee that every boss wants a dozen of. She was a dependable, hardworking, and extremely capable employee. Felicity was also well liked by the people around her. From a professional standpoint, Felicity was in a great place.

Many people are comfortable with the kind of situation that Felicity was in. Many people in the world are looking for a solid job with a dependable paycheck and a couple of weeks of vacation a year. Many people are content with that station in life. Being satisfied with that type of situation is fine for some people, but it falls far short for others. Felicity was not satisfied. When she mentally pictured her vision of the ideal life, it did not include getting up early every morning and rushing away from her family simply to gain the respect and approval of her bosses and coworkers. Felicity's vision of her ideal life centered on spending more time with her husband and children free from the financial constraints that kept them from doing the things they wanted to do.

Unfortunately, Felicity's life didn't look like her vision. Someone else (her bosses) determined her schedule. The sad truth was that Felicity's ideal life didn't look anything like the life she was living. This disparity between what Felicity had and what she wanted added up to a tremendous sense of dissatisfaction.

Today, Felicity's life is much different. She sets her own schedule, and as you can imagine, her schedule includes lots of mom time. Felicity still works. Her inner character gives her a desire to contribute to her family's financial needs. Today she is providing for her family's financial future with the help of her husband, Greg. Together they are actively involved in investing in real estate. Their real estate investing strategy provides them with enough positive cash flow to give them the financial freedom they enjoy. They have acquired and remarketed dozens of investment properties that produce a great passive income for their family. Their financial freedom gives Felicity the personal freedom to divide her time as she sees fit. Felicity's Dissatisfaction has been replaced by a sense of inner peace and fulfillment.

Fortunately for them, Adrian, Joe, and Felicity came to terms with their Dissatisfaction and used their inner unhappiness to motivate themselves to make some important changes. Imagine for a moment what Adrian's life would be like today if he hadn't taken action to make the Powerful Changes that he made. If Adrian chose not to take his Dissatisfaction seriously, he would still be overwhelmed by physical exhaustion. His family would still be dreaming of the day when he would be available to be the husband and father they need.

Or what if Joe hadn't taken his Dissatisfaction seriously? Not only would he still be working hard to make someone else wealthy, he would never be able to devote his time and financial resources to helping the human community through his charitable affiliations. Joe's life would still lack meaning and purpose, if he hadn't taken his Dissatisfaction seriously. If Felicity hadn't listened to her inner dissatisfaction, her children would still be missing out on all of the quality time that they now enjoy with their mother.

Dissatisfaction is a warning sign. It tells us that if we keep moving in the same direction in life, we could be headed for despair. Dissatisfaction is also the first step in the Powerful Changes Process. It is the beginning point that motivates people to make Powerful Changes in pursuit of their dreams. Adrian, Joe, Felicity, and thousands of John Burley's students began their journey toward fulfilling their dreams in the uncomfortable reality of Dissatisfaction. To their credit, they refused to medicate or mask their Dissatisfaction. They chose to do something about it by taking the next step in the Powerful Changes Process.

The Unhappiness Of Dissatisfaction

Before we move on to discuss that next step, let's pause for a moment and explore the emotional signs of Dissatisfaction. Every step or phase of the Powerful Changes Process is accompanied by a particular set of emotions. Identifying what these emotions are and comparing them to the emotions you are currently experiencing when you reflect on any given area of your life can give you the clues you need to determine where you are in the Powerful Changes Process.

Sometimes emotions are hard things to understand. We experience inner feelings and then often struggle to determine what those feelings are trying to tell us. At the same time, if we put in the effort to try to understand our inner emotions, they can be allies in our quest for self-understanding. Our emotions can give us the valuable insight we need in order to truly understand ourselves. This insight can empower us to make the adjustments we need to make in order to know true fulfillment and joy in life.

The staff members that John Burley recruits to help at his Advanced Investing Boot Camp all described a variety of emotions that they encountered as they moved through the Powerful Changes Process. The typical emotions that they described when talking about their inner Dissatisfaction included unhappiness, discontentment and in some cases borderline despair. Since these emotions have already been discussed in this chapter, we don't need to spend a lot of time on them at this point. At the same time, they do need to be looked at briefly in this context for the purpose of understanding what to look for in your inner life in order to determine if you are stuck in a state of Dissatisfaction.

Unhappiness and despair are the emotions that accompany Dissatisfaction in the Powerful Changes Process. Let's consider unhappiness for a moment. We've already seen that Dissatisfaction is an inner gnawing that prevents us from being at peace with the way things are. The emotion of unhappiness is an inner clue that helps us understand that we want more out of life than we are currently experiencing or enjoying. This unhappiness or restlessness invades our lives and keeps us from truly enjoying even the best of moments. In the midst of some of life's greatest moments, the emotion of nagging unhappiness will remind us that as soon as the joyful moment is over, we will be reminded that things could be even better if only our situation were a bit different or a bit more in line with our vision of a better life.

If ignored for too long, unhappiness can turn to despair. If our head tells us that life can be better than it is, but our hearts and hands never move in the direction of that better life, unhappiness can morph into its ugly evil twin – despair. As we've already seen, staying in despair for too long can lead to some very negative consequences in a person's life. Despair breeds depression. Despair is an utter loss of hope. In the Powerful Changes Process, despair rears its ugly head when we begin to believe that the unacceptable situation that we find ourselves in is never going to change. When a person begins to believe that their unsatisfactory life is "as good as it gets", the pain of despair can settle in and breed the cold, lonely feeling of depression.

Depression is a real problem in our world today. Studies show that the use of antidepressant medication is at an all time high. Some of the depression that people wrestle with is chemical in origin. In other words, for some reason some people's bodies do not produce enough of the natural hormones and endorphins that serve to stabilize their moods. The human body is an amazing creation. They human body has been equipped with a variety of coping mechanisms that help people deal with the stress and pressures of life. Occasionally, for a variety of reasons, someone's body will not be equipped with these chemical coping mechanisms that allow most people to stay balanced in their moods. The result is chemical depression. A doctor should treat these situations. Fortunately for people who suffer from chemical depression, science has come along way in the development of drugs that replace what the body cannot produce. So, some depression is chemical.

On the other hand, some depression is situational. In other words, some depression is brought on by difficult times in life or unacceptable situations. A person who experiences the loss of a loved one will often suffer from a bout with depression for a time. People often recover from these cases as they move through the stages of the grief process. Some situations, like an unfulfilling job or recognizing that life isn't what it could be, can lead to depression as well. This kind of situational depression can paralyze a life.

Depression can settle into a person's soul and totally take control of a life. The symptoms of depression are easily identified. Things like sudden inactivity, unexplainable sadness, and difficulty in concentration can be warning signs that a person is sinking into a state of depression. A significant increase or decrease in appetite or heightened sensitivity to feelings of rejection can also indicate that a life is being plagued by depression. A person who is depressed wants to sleep all day, avoid responsibilities and escape from the pressures of life in a variety of ways. Unhappiness can lead to despair, which can turn into depression if it is ignored for too long.

The bottom line of this is simple enough to understand. The emotions that accompany Dissatisfaction are unhappiness and despair. These emotions are the inner warning signs that tell us that something needs to change in our lives. No matter how hard we try to ignore these inner warning signs, they will normally not go away on their own. They will often keep knocking at the door of the heart until they either pound a hole in it or are taken seriously. And in the Powerful Changes Process, there is usually one last knock – one final pound – that gets the attention of the person experiencing Dissatisfaction. Let's turn our attention to that "Trigger Event" now as we try to understand the process that successful people go through as they make significant changes.

Action Steps

Before you move on to the next chapter, take a moment to go through these action steps.

Dissatisfaction is the first phase of the Powerful Changes Process. At the same time, Dissatisfaction is not something that you should try to manufacture in your life in an effort to move toward positive changes. You are either dissatisfied in a particular area of your life, or you're not. Getting the most out of the action steps in this book will require you to be completely honest with yourself.

Chances are pretty good that if you are reading this book, you are recognizing the need and desire you have to make some Powerful Changes in your life. Rather than try to duplicate the experience of someone that you will read about in this book, your Powerful Changes Process needs to accurately reflect where you are in your journey toward fulfilling your dreams. While the path that people take in the Powerful Changes Process is the same, the particulars and details of that path differ from person to person.

With that in mind, as you take these actions steps that are designed to tune you into your Dissatisfaction, simply be honest with yourself. Remember that Dissatisfaction comes in varying degrees of intensity depending upon what is valuable to you in life. Dissatisfaction can range from just a little feeling of unhappiness to major despair and even depression. It is also important to understand that Dissatisfaction in its early stages will not be as intense as it would be if it goes ignored for a prolonged period of time. These action steps are simply intended to help you avoid ignoring your Dissatisfaction so you can act on it before it might turn into full-blown despair.

1. Take a moment to think about the major areas of your life – the professional, spiritual, relational, physical, intellectual, and financial dimensions of your life. Reflect on where you are in these different areas of your life.

2. Now reflect on where you would like to be in each of these areas. It might be helpful for you to write a brief description of where you would like to be in each of these areas. This will allow you to really enter into this process. Ask yourself questions such as, "Where would I like to be financially at this point in my life?" or "Where would I like to be profes-sionally at this point?"

3. Now do a casual comparison between where you are and where you would like to be in these major areas of your life. In what area of your life is the distance between where you are and where you want to be the greatest?

4. Chances are pretty good that there is some disparity between where you are and where you want to be in certain areas of your life. Few people have completely "arrived" in every aspect of their lives. Without being too hard on yourself, begin to explore why the disparity exists. Are circumstances keeping you from moving forward in certain areas of your life? Is fear keeping you stuck in an unsatisfactory or unacceptable position? Is a lack of knowledge about how to move forward preventing you from making the progress you would like to make in the different facets of your life?

5. Without trying to fabricate emotions, ask yourself how you feel about the disparity between where you are and where you want to be in these areas of your life. Are you totally fine with this disparity? Are you dissatisfied and uncomfortable? When you reflect on the difference between where you are and where you want to be, do you feel like setting this book aside and ignoring the emotions that this process awakens in you? Are you mildly depressed about the disparity in your life or even severely depressed?

As stated earlier, the purpose of these actions steps is to help you avoid ignoring the Dissatisfaction that might exist in your life. This process is not designed to shame you or make you feel like you have failed in some way. Rather, the ultimate outcome of this process will be an increased sense of fulfillment and inner peace as you move through all of the action steps spelled out in this book.

Remember, Dissatisfaction is a warning sign that things aren't the way you wish they would be. Beyond that, it's important to remember that Dissatisfaction comes in varying degrees. What dissatisfies one person might not bother another person at all. However, being honest with yourself when it comes to any degree of Dissatisfaction that you might be experiencing can go a long way toward helping you find peace and fulfillment in life. Dissatisfaction is also the first step or phase in the Powerful Changes Process. It is certainly not the last step. You can make the changes you desire and realize the fulfillment of your dreams and goals in life. Be filled with hope at this point. You are moving in the right direction!

Chapter 3

Standing At The Crossroads of Life – The Trigger Event

The Truth About Trigger Events

The second step or phase in the Powerful Changes Process is the Trigger Event. There is an old expression that really captures the essence of the Trigger Event. The Trigger Event is the "straw that broke the camel's back". The idea behind this expression is easy enough to understand. Camels are the workhorses of desert countries. Throughout the history of the ancient near east on up through modern times, camels have been an important part of transportation and commerce in that part of the world. Camels are remarkably resilient animals. They can put up with a lot. Camels can endure harsh conditions. They can go for days without water. Camels can successfully navigate some of the most inhospitable terrain on Planet Earth. Camels are amazing survivors.

On top of all of that, camels can carry tremendous burdens. They can be piled high with cargo and supplies and be depended upon to carry that cargo through the harshest conditions imaginable.

So the idea, that one single piece of straw could finally break a camel's back seems ridiculous. At the same time, it captures the idea of pushing something too far. Picture a camel, loaded high with freight ready to embark on a caravan trip through the harsh climate of a dry, hot desert. The camel is loaded with the maximum weight it can possibly carry. Now imagine that the leader of the caravan decides to push the camel's weight limit one step further. He places one piece of straw on the camel's back, and that is the end of that. The maximum load has been exceeded. The camel can't even endure the addition of this tiny fraction of an ounce of weight. Its knees buckle, and the entire load comes crashing down. This was the straw that broke the camel's back. The straw pushed the camel past it's breaking point. That is why the expression "the straw that broke the camel's back" is such a perfect mental picture for understanding the essence of a Trigger Event.

A Trigger Event, in the Powerful Changes Process, is that last straw. It is the straw that breaks the back of a person loaded down with Dissatisfaction. It's the final event that causes all of the Dissatisfaction to come crashing down on the person who has been carrying its burden for too long. A Trigger Event is the final moment or event that pushes a person to take the necessary steps to transform what, to that person, is an unacceptable situation into a more fulfilling life.

A Trigger Event is a decisive moment that compels a person to step out of an unacceptable situation. It's the breaking point at which a person realizes that the pain of staying the same hurts more than the pain of moving forward into unknown territory. Put simply, a Trigger Event is the catalyst that prompts a person to take steps to *move out of* Dissatisfaction and *move toward* a better life.

The Trigger Event can be any event that serves as a catalyst to change the status quo. It is important to see the Trigger Event as a catalyst, because this imagery implies that the Trigger Event is a necessary step in making further progress toward fulfilling your dreams of a better life. Make no mistake about it; if a person is experiencing a prolonged period of Dissatisfaction, that Dissatisfaction will not go away on its own. The naïve idea that tells us that if we ignore a problem long enough it will eventually go away just isn't true. We can stuff the problem, but until it is truly resolved the problem will never go away. It will always exist until it comes to some kind of resolution. The Trigger Event is often the spark that ignites the resolution of Dissatisfaction. The Trigger Event is the culmination of Dissatisfaction in a moment of clarity and action.

A Trigger Event can be any experience that makes it apparent to a person that things must change right away. One of the most interesting things about the Trigger Event in the Powerful Changes Process is that it can take a variety of forms. Some of those forms can be positive events, like the birth of a child or graduation from college. Some of those forms can seem to be negative events, such as the death of a loved one or getting fired from a job. What triggers one person to make Powerful Changes might not necessarily trigger another person. In reality, every person is triggered to make positive changes in unique ways.

A Tragic Trigger Event

Here's an example of a negative event serving as the catalyst that led many people to make positive changes in their lives. The world will not soon forget the events of September 11, 2001. Like the assassination of President John F. Kennedy, most Americans can remember what they were doing when they found out about the horrible terrorist attacks that rocked the United States.

Until that point, terrorism had been something that Americans read about or watched on television. It had been the subject of action movies. Americans had even seen acts of terrorism perpetrated against their nation on foreign soil, such as the bombing of American embassies. However, an outside force had never attacked Americans on their own soil. Of course, in the years preceding the attack on the World Trade Center, extremist militia groups had attempted to attack America from within. The bombing of the federal building in Oklahoma City was a devastating event for the families who lost loved ones as well as all Americans who cherish security. However, nothing in collective past of the United States prepared Americans for the events of 9/11.

Americans and the entire world awoke that morning to horrible video images of a jetliner crashing into one of the Twin Towers. As people sat riveted to their television sets to gather any bit of information that might explain why such a thing happened, another jetliner came crashing into the second tower. From that moment on, there was no doubt that the explanation for these events was obvious. America was under attack.

Another plane crashed into the military headquarters of America, the Pentagon Building. Following that, a fourth jet was brought down in a field in rural Pennsylvania by brave passengers who had heard from their loved ones via cell phone calls that the high jacking of their plane was all part of a much larger and much more devious assault on the United States. By lunchtime on September 11, 2001 most Americans were numb with shock.

The impact of 9/11 on America and Americans cannot be quickly overlooked. Of course, those events changed the way Americans view themselves as a nation on the world scene. For the first time they became collectively aware that there are groups of people on this planet who hate America and their way of life for a variety of reasons. Those events certainly changed the way America now travels as a nation. Security in airports has been tightened beyond anything ever seen, and Americans don't mind. They understand the need for extra security now.

However, beyond the collective changes that have impacted Americans, the events of 9/11 have had a tremendous impact on individual values and life paths. In many ways, 9/11 served as an enormous Trigger Event that propelled many Americans to make drastic and significant changes in their lives. Some people resigned from jobs that consumed more of their time than they wanted to give so they could enjoy more time with their families. Many Americans willingly took a reduction in their standard of living so they could redirect their lives down a new path. Priorities were reset. Many people began to focus on the deeper spiritual issues of life that the busyness of their previous paths had crowded out.

The American armed forces experienced a surge of enlistment as many young people realized that the security they had hoped to enjoy in their later years might not exist if they didn't take action. 9/11 caused many Americans to reorganize their personal values. For many people, the focus shifted from "getting ahead" to "going deep". Many people started focusing on the lasting intangibles of life – things like relationships, spirituality, and inner peace – rather than focusing on the fleeting tangibles of acquiring stuff. The events of 9/11 served as a tragic Trigger Event that ultimately propelled many Americans to make positive changes in their lives.

On the home front of John Burley's team of dedicated Boot Camp staff members, the events of 9/11 compelled them to be more committed to spreading the message of financial freedom so that others might have the liberty of focusing on those intangibles.

John's staff members all related that 9/11 got their attention in a way that caused them to shift their ultimate goals and priorities in life. In fact, at the first Boot Camp that followed the events of 9/11, John Burley urged his volunteer staff members to step it up to meet the challenges that faced not only America, but the world, as a result of what had transpired just weeks before.

In the debriefing that followed the intensive five-day training event, John gathered his staff members around him and through heartfelt emotions encouraged them to understand that the work they were doing to train people to achieve their personal financial freedom was more important now than ever. John truly believes that the purpose of finding financial freedom is not simply to amass wealth so one can acquire stuff. John teaches his staff members and students to understand that the purpose of finding financial freedom is so that people can be more in control of their schedules and consequently focus on the important intangibles of life, such as family, friends, and charitable causes.

Without a certain amount of freedom in one's schedule, relationships and spiritual growth get set aside. Survival, keeping a job, meeting the ridiculous demands of a tyrannical boss – these are the things that work against a life that is focused on developing deep relationships and helping the human community. John reminded his staff members that their task was truly all about helping people find personal freedom so they could pursue the elements that are truly important in life.

In many ways, the events of 9/11 reveal the truth about Trigger Events. Trigger Events are significant events that serve as catalysts to greater change. Whether it is a positive event, like the birth of a child, or a negative event, like the tragedy of 9/11, Trigger Events cause people to look at the direction their lives are taking and make the necessary adjustments to move them toward a richer, more meaningful existence.

Very few events serve as collective Trigger Events the way the tragedy of 9/11 did. However, sometimes those large-scale world events do occur and cause a massive reevaluation of life paths. More often than not, Trigger Events are much more subtle and more uniquely tailored to the individual experiencing it. In other words, what triggers one person to make significant changes might not motivate another to make any progress at all in the Powerful

Changes Process. Trigger Events are as unique as the people who experience them. Let's take a look at some of the Trigger Events that compelled John Burley's Boot Camp staff members to step out of their discomfort zones and onto the path of the Powerful Changes Process.

Adrian Oakman's Trigger Event

You met Adrian Oakman in the last chapter. He was the discontented dairy farmer who was working harder than anyone should have to just to take care of his family. His life was weighed down by exhaustion and fatigue. Early mornings and late nights spent taking care of a large herd of dairy cattle kept him from focusing his energy on his family. His beautiful children were growing up before his eyes and he didn't have the time and energy he needed to be the involved father he wanted to be. Adrian's wife was holding the family together well, but the added strain of filling both parental roles was taking its toll on her.

The thing that needs to be understood about Adrian is that if he could have done more, he would have. He is a man who pushes himself to the limits. He is motivated by things like integrity, honor, loyalty, and responsibility. Life had boxed Adrian into an unacceptable situation. His days were spent on hard work. During his short nights his body struggled to recover from the energy expenditure of the day before.

Don't get the wrong impression about Adrian. He is no wimp. He is no physical weakling. Adrian is in great shape, and extremely athletic. One can't spend a life in manual labor and walk around with a lot of excess baggage. However, Adrian usually operated in an energy deficit. Exhaustion was his constant companion. One day it all came to a head.

Adrian had been granted the reprieve of a rare Saturday afternoon of rest. He had spent the morning tending to his dairy cows. After that exertion his body craved a moment of rest. He crawled into his bed and collapsed. As he lay there, Adrian could hear the sounds of his children playing in the yard. He so desperately wanted to join them, but he knew that if he was going to continue to provide for them, he needed to take advantage of the time he had to rest his body.

Then it happened. The happy noises coming from the yard turned into the sounds of an injured child. A small accident, nothing major, had happened as Adrian's children played that left one of them with a minor scrape. The cries of pain reached Adrian's ears. Adrian wanted to help his hurt child, but he knew that his wife would quickly get to the scene of the accident and take care of the situation. So Adrian opted to stay in bed and rest his weary body so that he could get up in an hour or so and get back to his farming chores.

Fortunately, Adrian's wife, Tracey, was there to tend to their child. And fortunately, the injury was nothing more than the kind of small scrape that most kids get from time to time while playing. However, that moment was Adrian's Trigger Event. That moment was the straw that broke the camel's back. It was a moment of clarity that brought all of the Dissatisfaction that he had been feeling crashing down on Adrian in a way that made him instantly realize that something had to change in his life. In that moment, Adrian understood that when a life path keeps a man so exhausted that he has to rest his fatigued body rather than tend to his injured child, then that man should choose another path if at all possible. At that moment in Adrian's mind, all of the Dissatisfaction and borderline depression that he had been dealing with for months came to fruition and triggered a major decision in his life. Adrian decided that he was going to make whatever changes were necessary so that he could get off the farm and into a more balanced life. Adrian wanted to find a career path that would allow him to spend his Saturday's in his yard playing with his children rather than being pinned to a bed by physical exhaustion.

Of course, Adrian did not have a clear idea of what he would do next. He didn't have a plan in place to replace his farming income. He loved farming. From the time he was a young boy he had envisioned himself as a farmer. Farming was all that Adrian knew and being a farmer brought a great deal of personal satisfaction to his life. However, the life of a dairy farmer was keeping Adrian from devoting his best waking hours to his family. Adrian simply knew that he was going to have to do something different. He made the decision to make a change.

The next few steps in the Powerful Changes Process led him to understand what that change would look like specifically. We'll discover those next few steps in the Powerful Changes Process in the next few chapters of this book. What is important at this point is understanding the dynamics of a Trigger Event. A Trigger Event is a decisive moment that compels a person to step out of what for that person is an unacceptable situation. That afternoon, as Adrian lay fatigued in bed listening to his hurt child cry, he experienced an internal Trigger Event that compelled him to make some changes. Gil's Trigger Event had the same effect on him.

Gil Barden's Trigger Event

Gil Barden is an active young man with an inner drive to excel. The thing that strikes people about Gil is his sheer determination to get the most out of his life. He enjoys pushing himself to do more and become more. There is not a lazy bone in Gil's body. He has always been an achiever.

When Gil began his career in the United States Navy, he pushed himself to become the best that he could possibly be. Gil saw himself as a career man in the Navy. Not only that, he aspired to become a U.S. Navy Seal. Navy Seal's are among the most elite soldiers in the world. Seals are a division of American Special Forces that are called upon to do some of the most challenging tasks imaginable in the military world.

Since that is the case, Navy Seals have to be trained to do many different tasks. Seals are often inserted into hostile territory and called upon to perform a variety of missions. Seals need to be proficient in a variety of skills in order to meet these challenges. One of the skills necessary for Seals is the ability to jump out of airplanes at low altitudes. These low altitude jumps are extremely dangerous and certainly not for the faint of heart. Of course, Navy Seals are not faint of heart. They are exceptionally brave and imminently qualified to carry out the tough jobs required of them.

So Gil was not at all fazed by his order to participate in a low-level jump training exercise. He had received these orders before from his commanding officer. He and his fellow soldiers were dispatched to a remote location in the Arizona desert to practice jumping out of aircraft at low altitudes. Gil's plane took off and reached the appropriate altitude. Gil and his fellow Seals lined up to jump. With precision timing and flawless accuracy, Gil and the rest of the Seals in his group followed orders. They jumped from the airplane one at a time without hesitation. Unfortunately, something happened next that would change Gil's life forever.

The drop site for the Seals was a small stretch of desert in southwestern Arizona. This site was chosen because of its remoteness and accessibility. Even though this piece of desert was remote, it was also accessible by a variety of paved roads. This kind of access was necessary so that the Seals could be retrieved by vehicle after they had executed their jumps.

As fate would have it, Gil and his fellow soldiers jumped out of their plane at the same moment a mid-size car was traveling down the road they were jumping near. The soldier who jumped immediately before Gil was in danger of colliding with the car as his descent passed over the road. He altered his route slightly to compensate. Since Seals jump in precision formation, this caused the other Seals to alter their courses of descent as well. Gil compensated. Unfortunately, this change in his descent pattern caused Gil to land on the asphalt road at a high rate of speed. As a result, Gil broke several bones in one of his feet and tore ligaments in both of his ankles.

The months of physical therapy that followed were grueling. Gil regained the use of his feet, but the injury made it impossible for him to function as a Navy Seal any longer. As mentioned earlier, Seals are called upon to carry out some physically demanding tasks. Gil's injuries left him unable to function at the level necessary for Navy Seals. In a single moment, Gil's life changed.

Trigger Events are like that sometimes. They sometimes come so suddenly and so unexpectedly that they fold the Dissatisfaction phase of the Powerful Changes Process into themselves and bring sudden change in an instant. In other words, sometimes the Trigger Event combines with Dissatisfaction to form a powerful moment that immediately changes the course of a person's life. More often that not, a period of Dissatisfaction precedes a Trigger Event. However, on some occasions the Trigger Event creates Dissatisfaction and compels a person to make massive life changes all in a single moment. That was the case for Gil.

From the moment Gil hit the pavement, he knew that his life would never be the same. However, what his new life would look like was a complete mystery to him at the time. Today, Gil Barden owns a thriving real estate investing business. He has acquired dozens of investment properties that provide him with a permanent passive income. He lives in San Diego, California and enjoys a fulfilling and meaningful life. Of course, Gil had no idea that his life would take such a turn for the better as he struggled to pick up the pieces of his life after his ill-fated jump. He would only discover and realize his vision of a better life as he moved through the subsequent steps of the Powerful Changes Process. We will turn to those steps soon, but first let's take a look at a few more noteworthy Trigger Events.

John Black's Trigger Event

John Black is a successful real estate investor in Australia. Like Gil, John owns a profitable real estate investing business that provides his family with a very comfortable passive income.

John's investment portfolio includes dozens of properties that generate positive cash flow. He has done very well for himself and his family as a successful real estate investor. Not only is John actively involved in buying and selling properties; he is also interested in helping other people realize the personal financial freedom that he enjoys. That is why John volunteers as one of the staff members at John Burley's Advanced Investing Boot Camp.

All of John Burley's volunteers are required to be active investors so they can have real world experience to pass on to students who are just learning about the world of real estate investing. At the same time, all of the staff members are required to have a passion to help people gain the knowledge they need while working through the emotional blocks that keep many people trapped in unacceptable situations for entirely too long. John Black meets those criteria. He is actively involved in investing and has a true passion to help people. However, John's life wasn't always as fulfilling as it is today.

Before John discovered his current life path, he was a respected engineer in Australia. He traveled all over the country doing what engineers do. He designed roads and bridges and reviewed construction plans for major projects. John's company flew him all over the country and often kept him away from home for extended periods of time. John was constantly rushing from one project to the next, moving from one place to another, in an effort to please his employers. The result was a lot of frustration and fatigue. John was unhappy.

John no longer enjoyed his life. He wanted something different – something that wouldn't keep him on the road so much. At the same time, engineering was all he had ever done. He didn't know what he would do to support his family if he gave up his career so, like a lot of people, John toughed it out. He hung in there and did his job well, and spent a lot of energy on ignoring his Dissatisfaction as much as he possibly could. However, his Dissatisfaction came knocking one day during an airplane flight in a way that caused John to experience his Trigger Event.

John had been on the road for days. In fact, he had been on six different airplanes in six days. That kind of traveling schedule can be grueling. John, who happens to be a tall man, had been crammed into coach seating as he traveled home from a long trip. He was worn out from the hard work and continuous travel. John was tired and wanted some rest, but as he sat in his cramped airplane seat and got bumped over and over again by the passenger sitting next to him and people walking up and down the aisle, he experienced his Trigger Event. A person can only be bumped so many times before he gets tired of it. John was getting knocked around in his uncomfortable seat. He got bumped one too many times that day. As a result, John experienced a Trigger Event.

Don't get the wrong impression. John is a man of high sophistication and well-developed self-control. He didn't act out on his inner frustration. He kept it in check. At the same time, all of the discomfort that he was experiencing on the outside caused all of the Dissatisfaction that he had been experiencing on the inside to come to fruition. Something triggered inside of John, and at that moment he decided that he was going to make some changes in his life. John decided that he no longer wanted to do what he was doing. He was no longer willing to travel in cramped airplanes, spend so much time on the road, and be deprived of his family for days on end.

In that moment John decided that he was going to begin to explore other options in life. Sure he wanted to take care of his family and be a good provider, but he didn't want to do that at the expense of living a miserable existence for the rest of his days. At the moment of his Trigger Event, when he got bumped one too many times, John decided that he was unwilling to trudge through an unhappy life while sucking up the misery that he felt inside. At the moment of his Trigger Event, John decided that he was going to make some changes.

People who are honest enough with themselves to recognize their internal dissatisfaction open themselves up to experience Trigger Events. Many people are content to ignore their inner discord. Many people believe that fulfilling lives are a luxury only afforded to those born into wealth and position. As a result, the vast majority of people in the Free World resign themselves to holding down jobs they don't like so they can get a couple of weeks of vacation a year if they are lucky. Too many endure fifty weeks every year so they can really live during the two weeks of vacation that their "generous" employers "lavish" upon them for all of their hard work. As John sat scrunched up on an airplane being bumped and stepped on by people all around him, he decided that he wasn't going to live like that anymore. His outer discomfort caused his inner dissatisfaction to speak to his heart with clarity. That inner message was a cry for change and freedom. At the moment of his Trigger Event, John decided that something had to change.

Steve Dover's Trigger Event

We met Steve Dover in the introduction of this book. Steve was the faithful employee for a large Australian company who as a boy had dreamed of growing up to become a millionaire businessman. Steve had grown up in a financially tight situation. His father had worked hard to provide for Steve and his brothers and sisters. The cost of raising a family and the restriction of the family's small income left very little money for more than simple survival. As Steve grew up and saw how hard his father worked for so little, he decided that he was going to do everything in his power to become financially independent.

Steve took the path that society told him would lead to his dream of financial freedom. He got a decent job with a large company and worked hard to excel. Steve was a top producer in his company. He had a great work ethic and put in long hours that made his company a lot of money. Steve's bosses loved him. He was bringing a steady stream of income into their coffers that far exceeded their expectations. They paid Steve a decent salary, but it in no way proportionately compared to the amount of revenue he was creating for his company. Somewhere along the way Steve began to realize that his bosses weren't really all that concerned about his personal success. A nagging sense of Dissatisfaction began to grow in Steve that caused him to recognize that if he worked himself to death, his employers would not necessarily care. Harder work didn't bring Steve more pay. Innovative thinking didn't bring him more promotions. Steve's employers had him right where they wanted him – making lots of money for the company so they could give themselves annual salary increases and cushy bonuses.

It is often painful to realize that the path you are walking on doesn't lead to where you want to go. Steve Dover had followed the traditional advice of society. He dreamed of being a millionaire businessman. Society told him to get a decent job, work hard, get promoted, receive profit sharing benefits and watch the millions come rolling in. So that's what Steve did. He got the decent job, worked hard, but none of the things that lead to lasting wealth ever materialized for Steve. He was beginning to see that society's advice was full of holes. In fact, Steve was beginning to see that the myth of becoming financially free and enjoying a comfortable retirement by working hard for a company was most likely perpetrated upon the public by high level executives who wanted misguided people to work hard so they could keep the bulk of the profits for themselves. This mental clarity was breeding the seeds of Dissatisfaction in Steve. All of this Dissatisfaction came crashing in during one moment of clarity that compelled Steve to change the direction of his life forever.

One day, all of Steve's feelings and suspicions about his employers simply looking out for themselves while overlooking all of his hard work were proven to be true in a remarkable way. Steve's company was going through a period of major restructuring after purchasing another company. Company executives decided that the systems of the new company needed to be merged with the older company to create the best possible situation. As a result, all of the offices were moved to a new larger location where the previous employees could work alongside the new employees. Steve arrived at the new office building that first day anxious to see what his new working conditions would look like. He couldn't have been more disappointed.

As Steve stepped into the office building he noticed that his employers had chosen to situate all of their employees in one large work area. Each employee's workspace was separated by a temporary office cubicle. Not exactly ideal working conditions, but Steve knew he could cope. However, one thing pushed him to the breaking point. Steve found his cubicle. It was fairly standard. It had three walls, a built in desk, and a simple cabinet connected to the top of the wall. However, Steve noticed something that troubled him. As he looked across the room at the cubicles that were filling up with new employees, Steve realized that the only difference between his cubicle and the cubicles of the brand new employees was that his had a cabinet and theirs didn't.

Years of hard work, producing big profits for his bosses, towing the company line, and all he had to show for it was a cabinet. This visual representation of the futility of all of his hard work was all that Steve needed in order to experience his Trigger Event. As he compared his cubicle – the cubicle of a dedicated employee who had made sacrifices for his company for years – with the cubicle of the brand new employee across the floor from him, Steve understood that continuing down his chosen path was just not going to get him where he wanted to be. Steve wanted to be a millionaire businessman. All he had to show for years of hard work was a lousy cabinet. This moment of clarity was Steve's Trigger Event.

Sometimes all it takes to experience a Trigger Event is seeing a concrete picture of what your heart suspects is true. In Steve's case, he suspected that his chosen path was not moving him toward the fulfillment of his dreams. When he saw that the only difference between his workspace and the workspace of the newest employee of the company was a cubicle, he knew for certain that his suspicions were true.

Remember, a Trigger Event is the catalyst that prompts a person to take steps to *move out of* Dissatisfaction and *move toward* a better life. Steve's catalyst was this concrete visualization of his inner suspicions. From that moment on, Steve Dover began exploring other options that would lead him toward his childhood dream of becoming a millionaire businessman. A few short years later, Steve was able to fulfill his dream. Today he is a millionaire businessman and much, much more. The path he took that led him to fulfill his dreams is an interesting story in itself. We will look at it in an upcoming chapter. First, let's see how another concrete visualization of an inner suspicion led one man to step out of his discomfort zone toward a better life.

Bryan Fergus' Trigger Event

Bryan Fergus' Trigger Event story is only slightly different from the rest. By now you have noticed some common themes in these Trigger Events. Many of the stories involve people who feel a bit trapped in a career that keeps them from focusing on their relationships with their family members and friends. Many of the stories center around people with a good work ethic who aren't afraid of work, but simply want to have the freedom to do what they want to do with the days they have been given. Bryan's Trigger Event story contains these same elements. The only real difference between Bryan's story and the stories that have been shared in this chapter already is the nature of Bryan's chosen path in life. When Bryan experienced his Trigger Event he had already spent his entire adult life up to that point serving the human community by being the minister of a large church in the metropolis of Phoenix, Arizona.

Bryan had grown up with a real sense of calling and purpose in his life. From his early teen years, he knew that he wanted to devote his life to helping people find personal peace and lasting joy through rich spiritual experiences. Bryan went to college to pursue a divinity degree so that he would be equipped to answer the deep questions that people have about the spiritual life. Bryan excelled in his area of expertise. Beyond that he had a passion and proficiency for ancient languages that allowed him to interpret sacred texts in accurate but meaningful ways for the people of his congregation.

Bryan became the head pastor of a struggling church in the Phoenix area at the age of twenty-five. Bryan and his wife, Debi, poured their hearts and souls into helping this little local group of spiritual seekers develop spiritually deep lives. Bryan walked with these people through the major moments of their lives. He married them when they fell in love with each other and buried them when they past from this life to the next. He helped confused parents deal with angst filled teenagers. He helped retiring men cope with the prospect of stepping out of professionally challenging lives into a life that no longer carried a title. Simply put, Bryan spent his energy on trying to help people thrive during the seasons of their lives.

In the midst of carrying out this important work, Bryan became the father of three children and pursued a graduate degree in theological studies. After receiving his Master of Divinity degree, Bryan was called upon to teach other men and women who were pursuing a similar direction in their lives. So, beyond being the head pastor of what had now become a large and thriving church, Bryan was now spending his time and energy on being an adjunct professor at a graduate school in the Phoenix area.

To the outsider, everything looked fine. Bryan was a respected and successful minister and a budding professor. However, to an insider things looked out of balance. Only Bryan's wife, Debi, and a few close friends understood the extreme demands that such a life placed on Bryan. Ministers are "on call" twenty-four hours a day, seven days a week, three hundred sixty five days a year. While Bryan had some help when it came to carrying out the programs of the church he pastored, his church members still needed a large amount of his time and energy. Beyond that, preparing to speak to his congregation and teach his classes as well as handling all of the administrative demands of a large and growing church, typically demanded sixty-five to seventy hours of his time each week.

This grueling schedule left little time for Bryan to focus on the young family that he had at home. The fact of the matter was that this grueling schedule really left little time for Bryan to do anything beyond meeting the demands of his different positions. Bryan's three children were growing up before his eyes. His wife, Debi, was forced to fill both parental roles while Bryan met the professional demands and challenges laid out before him. Beyond that, Bryan was exhausted. The physical and emotional demands of being a minister, teacher, and conference speaker were taking a toll on him. Bryan knew that something needed to change.

Today, Bryan will tell you that he struggled with knowing how to balance all of the responsibilities placed before him. He desperately wanted to help all of the people in his church as well as train other men and women to be skilled helpers of people as well. However, as Bryan's congregation grew the demands grew with it. Bryan struggled to say "no" when necessary. The result was what at times seemed like a never-ending string of tasks and challenges that demanded Bryan's attention. All the while, Bryan's two very young daughters and his infant son went without the attention from their father that they needed in their formative years. Bryan knew that his life was out of balance. He knew that something needed to change. In fact, Bryan had tried to remedy the situation on numerous occasions, but was unable to find a working solution.

One evening, Bryan experienced a Trigger Event that put his situation in perspective in a way that nothing else could. Bryan came home very late from his office that evening. For some reason, Bryan's two daughters, ages three and five, were still awake. In fact, they were sitting on the sofa watching television while Bryan's wife, Debi, tended to their infant son. As Bryan stepped through the front door and into his living room, his young daughters looked up at him. Bryan will remember the look they gave him for the rest of his life. As they looked up from their television program, Bryan's little girls looked at their father as if he were a stranger. Bryan could tell that for an instant their little minds were trying to process who this strange man was who had come walking through their front door. Of course, they very quickly recognized their father and ran to give him hugs. But their first reaction was confusion and even fear. At that moment, Bryan realized that his grueling schedule and lack of balance had made him a stranger in his own home. Bryan's daughters were unfamiliar with their father's presence.

At that moment, Bryan experienced an inner Trigger Event. It became very clear to him that something needed to change. He vowed that he would no longer sacrifice the needs of his family for the sake of helping others. He knew he needed to make the necessary changes to restore balance and regain perspective in his life. As often happens, it took some months before a series of events brought the needed changes to Bryan's life. However, that late night encounter with his confused daughters served as the Trigger Event that altered the course of Bryan's life forever.

Trigger Event stories are all remarkably similar. They all relay how an instant of mental clarity or a life-altering event can bring Dissatisfaction into focus so that a person can begin to make the necessary changes that will lead to a more fulfilling life. It should be obvious from the Trigger Event stories detailed in this chapter, that the details of Trigger Event stories are as unique and varied as the people who experience them. Again, that is simply because every person's life situation is unique. What motivates one person might not motivate another. However, when a person reaches a breaking point – when Dissatisfaction becomes so unbearable that Powerful Changes need to take place – quite often the result is a Trigger Event of such magnitude that maintaining the status quo is out of the question. After a person experiences a real Trigger Event, the discomfort of staying the same becomes more painful than the discomfort of moving into new territory.

A Trigger Event is a decisive moment that compels a person to step out of an unacceptable situation. A Trigger Event serves as a catalyst to change the status quo. For that reason it is necessarily the second step or phase in the Powerful Changes Process. When a life begins to recognize an inner sense of dissatisfaction, something has to happen to spur that life to do something about that inner sense of unhappiness. That is the function that the Trigger Event serves. In the Powerful Changes Process, the Trigger Event is the straw that broke the camel's back. It is the breaking point that compels a person to change.

The Agitation And Anger Of Trigger Events

Like every phase of the Powerful Changes Process, the Trigger Event is characterized by distinct emotions. The first phase in the process, Dissatisfaction, is characterized by unhappiness and even despair. More often that not, the Trigger Event phase of the Powerful Changes Process is categorized by agitation of anger. These are the words that best serve to capture the array of emotions that surround the Trigger Event phase of a life change.

When the calm waters of a person's inner life are disturbed for whatever reason, he or she will experience an emotion that can best be described by the word "agitation". Agitation is an inner sense of unsettled disturbance. Of course, positive Trigger Events like the birth of a child or graduating from college are usually accompanied by a positive kind of agitation that moves a person into new territory in life. However, when it comes to experiencing a Trigger Event that pushes a person to move away from Dissatisfaction, this inner sense of agitation often takes a different spin and eventually manifests itself in anger.

When the final straw is loaded upon the camel's back and the weight of Dissatisfaction comes crashing down, quite often the person going through the Powerful Changes Process experiences an inner surge of **anger**. For instance, as Adrian Oakman lay in his bed listening to the sounds of his injured child, he felt a growing sense of anger over his position in life. His inner sense of agitation manifested itself in anger. As John Black got bumped over and over again after being on six different airplanes in six days, his inner sense of agitation developed into a growing feeling of irritation. This sense of irritation resulted in a low level of anger.

It's important to understand that anger is a secondary emotion. In other words, anger never comes out of nowhere. It is always an inner reaction to another feeling. For instance, when a person loses a loved one, one of the emotions that is often experienced in the grief process is anger. But anger is really nothing more than a reaction to the incredible sense of loss and pain that most people feel when they lose anything that is precious to them. In the Powerful Changes Process, anger is an emotional reaction to the Dissatisfaction that piles up during the first phase in the process. Here's an easy way to look at it. When the pain of Dissatisfaction becomes overwhelming, a person often gets angry over the inner pain, unhappiness and discomfort caused by this dissatisfaction. When all of the factors of life come together to form a Trigger Event, a person finally gets "mad enough" to change. For that reason, the emotion that is most closely related to the Trigger Event phase of the Powerful Changes Process is anger.

Action Steps

Before you move on to the next chapter, take a moment to go through these action steps.

Like Dissatisfaction, Trigger Events can't be manufactured. They just happen. At the same time, chances are pretty good that you have experienced a variety of Trigger Events over the course of your life as you have grown and developed as a person. Maybe you have changed careers more than once during your life. Maybe you moved out of one neighborhood into a new neighborhood for a variety of reasons. Whatever changes you might have made over the course of your life, it's important to recognize that something triggered those actions that have certainly changed your life forever.

Or maybe you are already on the path to a life change. Maybe you have been loaded down with Dissatisfaction for years. Maybe you experienced a Trigger Event that has already moved you into the Search phase of the Powerful Changes Process. We'll discuss the Search phase of the Powerful Changes Process in depth in the next chapter of this book. Maybe your Trigger Event is still fresh in your mind. Maybe it happened last month or even last week, and you have picked up this book because you want to better understand what is happening to you.

Since we have all experienced Trigger Events at some level that have shaped the course and direction of our lives, it will be helpful to take some time to reflect on those Trigger Events. Take a moment and work through these actions steps as you gain a better understanding of the Powerful Changes Process and how to put it to work to achieve your vision of a better life.

1. Take some time to read through the Trigger Event stories in this chapter one more time. As you read, try to enter into the stories recorded. Imagine that you are Adrian or Gil or John or Steve or even Bryan. What feelings would you be experiencing if you were in their shoes at the moment of their Trigger Events?

2. Which Trigger Event stories come the closest to describing your inner feelings when you experienced a Trigger Event moment in your life?

3. Reflect on your life. Try to remember a time in your life when you experienced a similar pivotal moment. Enter into that experience again. What happened – in detail? What were you feeling inside when events finally triggered you to make significant changes?

4. Have you experienced a Trigger Event in your professional career? Have you experienced a Trigger Event moment in a relationship? Have you experienced a Trigger Event in your spiritual development? If so, think about the factors that converged to make that moment so significant in your life. Take a moment to list those factors.

Trigger Events are decisive moments that compel people to step out of what they consider to be unacceptable situations. However, taking that first step out of a discomfort zone can be a bit intimidating. As a person moves out of an unacceptable situation, he or she begins a Search process. This Search is a quest to discover and obtain a more acceptable and even ideal situation. All of the members of John Burley's Advanced Investing Boot Camp staff went on Searches that eventually led them to fulfill many of their life dreams by achieving personal financial freedom. Let's turn our attention to this important and necessary step of the Powerful Changes Process in the next chapter. Let's talk about The Search.

Chapter 4

There Must Be A Better Way

Simply Searching

For the past century, people have been combing the Superstition Mountains directly east of the Greater Phoenix Metropolitan area in the great state of Arizona searching for the Lost Dutchman's Gold Mine. Legend has it that a reclusive prospector found a huge vein of gold in the mountains that now loom over the east side of what Arizonans call "The Valley of the Sun". This prospector, a man named Jacob Waltz, would period- ically slip off into the Superstition Mountains and return to Phoenix with a bonanza of gold ore. He would live on the proceeds of his gold until it ran out, then Waltz would make another trip to his mine, braving threats from hostile Apache Indians, and those interested in discovering his cache of precious metal.

The time was the late 1800's and the Valley of the Sun was a strange place to be. The Earps and their friend Doc Holliday were stirring up trouble in the legendary town of Tombstone, Arizona a few hundred miles south of Phoenix. Geronimo, the brave Apache warrior and chief, was determined to keep his people from falling prey to the ravages of the strange intruders that had overrun their land. Geronimo's exploits carried him back and forth through the mountains and canyons of Arizona as well into other surrounding territories. Geronimo's raiders often found themselves traveling through the Superstition Mountains.

In spite of these risks and the many others associated with the wild, wild West, Jacob Waltz made several trips into the Superstition Mountains where he would load up with gold and return to his home an even richer man. It seemed to casual observers that Jacob's payload of gold never ran out. As many trips as he made into the mountains, Jacob always came home loaded down with the precious yellow stuff. Time and time again curious and greedy opportunists would stake out Jacob's home until he left on another journey into the Superstition Mountains. They would do their best to follow Jacob's path. However, Jacob was shrewd and smart and never took the same path twice. No one was ever able to follow Jacob Waltz to the location of his gold mine. In fact, many would-be stalkers never returned from their quest to find Jacob's legendary horde of gold.

Jacob carried the secret of the location of his abundant gold mine to his grave. Upon his death, people scrambled to find any clue that would lead them to Waltz's never-ending supply of gold. A map was eventually discovered, supposedly drawn by Jacob's own hand, but the details and landmarks on that map are vague enough that it has provided little help in determining the location of Jacob's horde of gold. It's as if Jacob Waltz never wanted anyone to discover the bonanza that made him a very wealthy man. Even in death, Jacob has kept his coveted secret. However, that hasn't stopped people from searching for it.

Over the decades since his death, hundreds of people have wandered into the Superstition Mountains searching for the Lost Dutchman's Gold Mine, as Jacob's stash has come to be known. Some have speculated that Jacob never really had a mine of gold at all. Some believe that Jacob merely found a forgotten horde of gold hidden in the Superstition Mountains by marauding Apaches who had confiscated the gold from Mexican miners and carried it north to the Arizona Territory.

Some theorize that the gold was stashed in the Superstitions by the Spanish explorer, Peralta, as he journeyed up through Mexico and into the budding United States. This theory suggests that as Peralta journeyed northward laden with gold from his previous expeditions, he left a large cache of gold in the Superstitions thinking that he would continue on his journey northward in search of more treasure. Peralta didn't count on encountering the Apaches who massacred his men as they were preparing to leave the area in 1847.

Regardless of the source of the gold, whether it was an actual mine or a large stash left by someone, evidently Jacob Waltz found it and took advantage of his discovery. People have been trying to rediscover what Jacob found so many years ago. Some believe that the stash that Jacob discovered simply ran out. This would seem to explain why his cache of gold has not been found to this day. Others believe that the gold is still out there somewhere, waiting to be found and waiting to make someone an incredibly wealthy person. So, people regularly venture into the Superstition Mountains searching for the Lost Dutchman's Gold Mine. They hope to strike it rich and spend their lives in wealth and luxury. When they step into the domain of the Superstition Mountains, they are really searching for a better life.

Every Positive Change Involves A Search

Think of all of the Searches or quests that people have undertaken through the centuries. A quest prompted Christopher Columbus to head west from Spain in search of a better trade route to India. The result of his Search was the discovery of what he called, the "New World". Today that New World is home to hundreds of millions of people. Lewis and Clark, the legendary frontier explorers started out on a search for a water way that cut across the heart of the United States of America. As they trudged across rugged terrain and encountered danger at every turn they opened up the American West.

Beyond searches for new lands, people have undertaken some amazing searches that have resulted in tremendous discoveries. People have searched for the cures to diseases that have virtually eradicated illnesses from the planet that once ended lives by the thousands.

When people are looking for a better way to do something or the better life that comes with the discovery of something like a hidden treasure, a Search always precedes discovery. For that reason, every major change that people experience in life includes some kind of a Search process.

As Bryan interviewed John Burley's Boot Camp staff members, he discovered that a common phase or step that they went through in their Powerful Changes Process could best be described as a

Search. After people endure the Dissatisfaction that often builds up and comes to a head in the form of a Trigger Event, they necessarily begin a Search that will lead them in the direction of the better life that they are seeking. People don't immediately step from a Trigger Event experience into the better life that they dreamed of. They go through a process that begins with a Search to discover a path that will lead them down the road toward the fulfillment of their dreams.

But the Search is more than simply a quest to discover an avenue or vehicle for realizing a set of personal goals or a personal vision of a better life. The Search also involves discovering those goals and painting a picture of the ideal life that the seeker is after. In the Search phase of the Powerful Changes Process, a person begins to evaluate life priorities, personal goals, and even past lifestyle choices in an effort to get in touch with what he or she really wants out of life. During this phase of the Powerful Changes Process, a person begins to fantasize about an ideal life as though it were an achievable reality. He or she paints a mental picture of what that ideal life looks like. He ponders things like where he would live if he could live anywhere that he wanted to. He even begins to think about what type of lifestyle he would choose if all of the choices were up to him. So the Search is about more than just figuring out a path that will enable a person to arrive at a better life. The Search also involves coming to terms with what that better life would truly look like.

During the Dissatisfaction phase of the Powerful Changes Process, people begin to realize that there must be a better life than they are experiencing. They might even think about the uncomfortable elements in their lives that they would like to change if they could. For instance, in a state of dissatisfaction a person might dream about being his own boss so that he wouldn't have to deal with his unpleasant boss anymore. Or a dissatisfied person might dream about leaving an unhealthy relationship, knowing that there has to be a better match out there. However, once a Trigger Event happens, the dissatisfied person becomes the seeker.

Once the Search begins, the seeker starts to look at the other side of the coin of unpleasantness. Instead of just fantasizing about not having to deal with his cranky boss anymore, the seeker begins to envision a situation in which he has reached the place of either working in a solo career or even being the boss himself. As this vision of a better life begins to crystallize, the seeker begins the process of investigating possibilities. The seeker starts to explore options and even tries to picture what his life could be like if he chose any given option.

The Many Manifestations Of "The Search"

The truly interesting thing about the Search step in the Powerful Changes Process is the variety of forms that the Search itself can actually take. The Search might take the form of reading a book. In fact, you might be in the Search phase of your Powerful Changes Process right now. Reading this book might in fact be a part of your Search for a better way to live. Maybe you picked up this book hoping that it would give you some of the clues that would lead you in the direction of fulfilling your dreams. So, in a very real way reading this book might be the form that your Search is taking at this moment! John Burley's #1 internationally known, best-selling book, *Money Secrets of the Rich*, has been a part of the Search phase of the Powerful Changes Process that tens of thousands of people have accessed as they have moved toward a life of financial freedom. It's not uncommon for people to pick up a book or two as they begin to explore possible avenues that might lead them in the direction they wish to go.

The Search might even take the form of attending a seminar. John Burley speaks at a variety of events in the United States, Australia, and New Zealand. Quite often people attend his events, such as his Automatic Wealth Seminar, because they are looking for a way to increase and even restore their financial health. So in a very real way, attending this seminar is simply a part of the Search process that leads them toward a better life. In their Search for options that will lead them to financial independence, these people seek out the advice of financial experts. Since John is an internationally known authority on successful financial habits and innovative investment strategies, he often encounters people at his training events that are in the Search phase of the Powerful Changes Process.

Beyond deliberately seeking the advice of recognized experts, the Search can take less formal forms. Someone who is seeking options for a better life might casually mention the process that he is going through to a friend, not realizing that the friend has undertaken a similar Search in the recent past. In these cases, the Search simply takes the form of a deep conversation with a friend.

Some people turn to therapists or life coaches during the Search phase of the Powerful Changes Process. A few people are brave enough and smart enough to understand that it doesn't hurt to consult a trained expert who is adept at helping people explore their inner lives. These therapists and life coaches are able to bring clarity to inner thoughts, feelings and struggles as their clients explore their own inner emotions and the factors that have shaped their lives up to that point in time. Therapists and life coaches often bring insight that allows a person to speed up the Search phase of the Powerful Changes Process as they clarify their own desires and life goals under the guidance of a skilled student of human behavior.

The Search step in the Powerful Changes Process takes many forms. Searching for a path that will lead to a better life can be as informal as a casual conversation with a friend to the structured environment of a therapy session. The Search can involve reading a book, listening to a tape set, or stumbling across an article or advertisement in a magazine or a newspaper. Searching for the path to a better life can even include attending a seminar or training session in search of the answers to the problems that have created the need for a new path in life. Whatever form it takes, this step in the Powerful Changes Process is simply characterized by a hunger to find a path that will lead the seeker to life he or she craves.

As Bryan interviewed John Burley's team of volunteer Boot Camp staff members, they all described a period of searching for a path that would lead them toward achieving their financial goals. They all understood that once their financial goals were met they would then have the freedom they needed to pursue their life-long dreams. When John's staff members began their Search for a better life, they were all interested in this common goal. They all wanted to be able to achieve financial freedom and independence, so they all embarked on their own Searches for the path or door that would lead them to where they wanted to go. Of course, all of these staff members eventually discovered the financial strategies of John Burley and implemented them in remarkable ways that quickly led them to find this financial freedom. However, the paths that they took that led them to John's information were all unique. Let's briefly look at a few of their Search stories so we can see the dynamics of the Search process in action.

Jerry and Lisa Hoganson's Search

Jerry and Lisa Hoganson are a dynamic couple from the northern United States. They grew up in a typical small town American environment. They fell in love with each other, got married and settled into a typical middle class lifestyle. Jerry worked a blue-collar job and Lisa pursued her own career. Their goals were modest at first. They simply wanted to spend their days together in happiness and peace. However, their lives didn't stay typical.

Jerry and Lisa began to realize that there is more available out there in the world than a mere "average" existence. Because they are filled with energy and a strong desire to get the most out of life, Jerry and Lisa quickly became dissatisfied with their typical lives. A freak accident on a piece of heavy equipment was the Trigger Event that Jerry needed to move him out of his average, dissatisfied life into the Search phase of the Powerful Changes Process. Fortunately, Jerry escaped any major injury, but his escape was narrow enough that it propelled him to look for another line of work that would insure his safety so that he would be around to take care of Lisa and their growing family.

Jerry began to Search for a way to achieve his financial freedom. He wanted to create enough passive income so that he could eventually retire young and focus his energy on the passions of his life. Passive income is simply income that a person receives from investments or even royalties in some cases. For example, John Burley is an avant-garde real estate investor. He purchases a home for investment purposes, turns around and remarkets it to a new occupant who pays him more than the underlying mortgage on the home. The difference between the mortgage and what John receives from the new occupant is the spread. John doesn't work for this spread each month. It just passively comes to him because of his investments strategies. This is passive income, and Jerry and Lisa wanted a steady stream of it coming into their bank accounts so they could achieve their own financial goals. As a result, Lisa willingly supported Jerry in his efforts to move in a new direction.

Jerry began to listen to tape sets featuring motivational speakers. These tape sets encouraged Jerry to believe in himself enough to pursue his dreams. Although people around Jerry told him that life was all about getting an average job and settling down to an average life so that he could enjoy an average retirement, Jerry instinctively knew that there is more to life than being average. Jerry continued to coach himself by listening to tape sets. Along the way he began reading books that started offering him more than just belief in himself. The books that Jerry got his hands on convinced him that there were systems and very real strategies available that could help him create the passive income he desired for his family.

One of these books encouraged Jerry to begin to dabble in the field of investing in real estate. He ventured into this unknown territory and realized that it had potential. At the same time, Jerry knew that his Search wasn't over. He needed more information. So Jerry signed up for a seminar. It just so happened that John Burley was scheduled to be a featured speaker at this seminar. When Jerry heard John speak, he realized that he had Discovered the Door that would lead him to achieve his financial goals and dreams for his family.

Today, Jerry and Lisa are extremely successful real estate investors. They have adapted a cash flow strategy in real estate investing that enables them to remarket mobile homes for a substantial passive profit. Jerry and Lisa have acquired and remarketed dozens of investment properties that provide them with a very large stream of passive income. They have moved toward their dream of total financial freedom, and will certainly achieve that dream while they are still young and full of unbridled energy.

Take note of the basic elements of the Search that Jerry and Lisa embarked upon. It started with a tape set here and there. It then moved them toward a few books that caused them to dabble in an area that might possibly move them toward financial freedom. One of the books ultimately led Jerry to a seminar, where he heard John Burley lay out simple and easy-to-follow strategies for creating positive cash flow through investing in real estate. Jerry and Lisa chose to implement these strategies, and today they are well on their way to fulfilling their dreams. From tapes to books to dabbling to a seminar, the Search that Jerry and Lisa made led them to the path to achieving their goals.

Adrian Oakman's Search

We have been following Adrian Oakman's story through the steps of the Powerful Changes Process because it clearly illustrates the different steps people take as they move toward lasting change. We've already seen how discontented he was with the life of a dairy farmer in New Zealand. We've entered into his Trigger Event story and been able to empathize with him as a father and husband who wanted nothing more out of life than to be able to be more available to his wife and children. Adrian's Search story also deserves to be told.

Upon experiencing his Trigger Event, Adrian began to apply common sense to his situation. He quickly realized that the reason he was working so hard was simply because he wanted to provide his wife and children with a comfortable lifestyle. Adrian began to realize that there must be an easier way to make a living out there than being a dairy farmer. Adrian's strong work ethic and level head led him to discover that if he wanted to be financially independent, he needed to seek mentors among people who had already achieved the lifestyle and financial freedom he sought.

Discovering mentors is often an important element in the Search process. The great thing about mentors is that they can take many forms. Some mentors are found among the dead. As we read biographies or encounter quotes from great men and women of the past, we can incorporate their philosophies and values into our lives and adopt them as our own. So in a very real sense, we can find mentors among the dead.

We can find mentors among the living as well. As we establish relationships with wise and successful men and women we can "adopt" them as role models. We can emulate their lives and adapt the wisdom they share with us to meet the unique demands of our individual situations. At the same time, we don't necessarily need to know people personally in order to embrace them as mentors. We can admire them from afar, read what they have written, listen to what they have said, and as a result receive mentoring from them.

Throughout his Search, Adrian found mentors among the living, though he personally knew very few of them. Like the Search that Jerry and Lisa undertook, Adrian began to listen to tape sets and read books in an effort to discover his path to financial health and freedom. Along the way, Adrian stumbled upon a tape set that John Burley had produced that introduced him to the possibilities of creating passive income and positive cash flow through investing in real estate. Adrian began to see that his Search for a money mentor had led him to someone who might be able to provide the answers he needed so that he could not only find financial freedom but also discover a way to be more available to his wife and children.

Adrian's Search for a path to a better life began to have a sense of urgency when he realized that the financial resources he was pouring into his Search were quickly depleting his financial reserves. Sometimes searching for the path that will lead to a better life requires a substantial personal commitment. Sometimes the Search requires a great deal of time or even money. Sometimes the Search requires brutal honesty with ourselves as we come to terms with who we are as people and what we are really capable of accomplishing. There is always a cost involved in the Search phase of the Powerful Changes Process. Whether it requires financial resources or time, or even the emotional energy that gets spent when doing deep soul searching, the Search step in the Powerful Changes Process calls for people to fully enter into the experience and give whatever it takes to find a path that will lead them to greater fulfillment and meaning in life.

Adrian had allocated a set amount of money to investigating his options. He was searching for a new way to provide for the financial needs of his family that wouldn't require so much time and energy. He wanted to be able to pursue a career that wouldn't take everything out of him so that he could have something left over at the end of the day to offer to his family. Adrian's Search eventually led him to John Burley's information. Adrian invested in one of John Burley's tape sets that caused him to realize that his path to financial freedom and a fulfilling life would involve becoming a real estate investor.

While becoming a real estate investor is not the only path that can lead a person to a life of financial freedom and personal fulfillment, Adrian's Search showed him that this particular path would meet the criteria for the type of life that he wanted to live.

Adrian's Search was a relatively short process. Sometimes the Search process can take much longer. Adrian's Search eventually led him to the door that opened onto a better life. The whole point of the Search is taking the time to do the inner and outer exploration that will lead to personal meaning and fulfillment. Adrian did that hard work and today he is living his dream.

Dean Edelson's Search

Dean Edelson is a very likeable guy. People who spend time around Dean know that they will do a lot of smiling and laughing in his presence. He has an amazing sense of humor and a genuine love and concern for people that causes them to drop their defenses and welcome his friendship. Dean's Search for a better life followed a period of unsettled wandering through life. As a young man Dean left a graduate school education behind to pursue a personal dream. He wanted a career in show business. Since Dean is just a naturally funny man, he pursued a career in comedy. Dean developed a stand-up comedy routine that he took on the comedy club circuit for years. He spent some time on cruise ships as a stand-up comedian entertaining passengers as they escaped from the cares of life. Dean enjoyed a good living and a measure of popularity that any comedian would be happy to embrace. However, constant travel and doing the same thing over and over again caused Dean to become bored and restless. He wanted more out of life than making people laugh on ships.

So Dean stepped away from a life as a performer to begin a new career as a film and television writer. He was looking for another way to get something worthwhile out of life. Along the way, Dean met Elaine, the love of his life. Elaine is a wonderful woman with a deep empathy for the inner feelings of others. Dean knew that in Elaine he had found his soul mate. They were eventually married and began a family together. As Dean continued to discover his life path, he never stopped looking for a fulfilling professional path that would enable him to provide for his family while pursuing his passion of writing. Dean took jobs as a freelance writer/producer in the Hollywood industry, enjoying a healthy measure of success.

At the same time, Dean and Elaine became weary of the Hollywood scene. They had moved to southern California so that Dean could pursue his screenwriting career. Dean's amazing sense of humor and his sharp mind allowed them to make a good living. But anyone who has ever lived in the Greater Los Angeles Area knows that for many people the constant pressure of huge crowds of people, poor air quality, maddening traffic, and a high cost of living can rob a life of joy and peace. Dean and Elaine wanted joy and peace in their lives. So Dean mounted another Search.

Dean's Search story up to this point illustrates an important point. As you've read through an abbreviated look at his life in the previous few paragraphs, you have no doubt noticed that

Dean has embarked upon several Searches throughout the course of his life. Dean started out in college and then graduate school to pursue a certain life path. When he became aware that his course of action was not going to bring him the meaning and purpose that he was looking for in life, Dean stepped into another journey through Powerful Changes Process. Dean's career in show business met a need that he had for a time, but as he grew and developed as a human being, more changes became necessary. So he once again recognized his Dissatisfaction, experienced a Trigger Event, and began a Search process that led him to the most fulfilling human relationship he has ever enjoyed – his marriage to Elaine.

As Dean and Elaine began to develop and evolve as a couple, and as they brought a beautiful little daughter into the world, they both became aware of a certain amount of dissatisfaction that centered on Dean's career and their life together in southern California. This Dissatisfaction led to a Trigger Event, which ultimately led to another Search.

People progress through many changes during the course of their lives. The simple reason for this is that most people continue to grow and develop as human beings. Priorities change, new experiences enter the mix, and the need for change becomes apparent. The truth is that life is a progression of change. Understanding the process of change equips us to understand what we are going through. Understanding the Powerful Changes Process also empowers us to successfully navigate the waters of change without running aground on stagnant frustration or being overwhelmed by a storm of anxiety.

As Dean embarked upon another Search in the evolution of his life, he became aware of the power of passive income to provide his family with the freedom that they desired in life. Dean stumbled upon a book that made him aware of the possibility of becoming financially free. Freedom is important to Dean and Elaine. More than anything, they want to be able to determine their own destinies in life. The thought that he could acquire assets that would passively generate a permanent income for his family resonated with Dean. So he began to seek out people who had pursued this path.

One evening, Dean went to an informal gathering of beginning investors. As Dean talked with people who were expressing similar passions, one of the members of the group causally mentioned a man whom Dean had never heard of before. That man's name was John Burley. As Dean engaged in this conversation with this member of an informal investment group, Dean discovered that John Burley had blazed a trail in creating passive income through innovative real estate investment strategies. As the basics of John's strategies were described to Dean, something clicked in his head. Dean perceived that he had stumbled upon the path that he had been searching for.

Dean's Search started with a book that led him to an informal investors meeting. At that meeting a chance encounter with someone who was familiar with John Burley's investment strategies and training opportunities was the encouragement that Dean needed to investigate a new course of action. Today, Dean and Elaine live in a beautiful town in central Arizona. They have the freedom to determine the direction of their lives. Dean has developed a flourishing portfolio of dozens of real estate investments that provide his family with the passive income they need to live a great life. Dean's Search clearly paid off.

The Fear Of Searching

Fear is one of the most common emotions known to mankind. The emotion of fear taps into our primitive sense of survival and urges caution when facing unknown adversaries. Fear can be a powerful force that can either cripple a life or compel it to move out of discomfort in search of something better.

For many, fear is the emotion most commonly associated with the Search phase of the Powerful Changes Process. As people come to terms with the unhappiness associated with the Dissatisfaction phase of the Powerful Changes Process, their emotional intensity builds up until a Trigger Event replaces that unhappiness with anger. Anger over their place in life and their mounting frustration with circumstances both within and beyond their control erupts into a Trigger Event moment. At the point of the Trigger Event, a person realizes that he can never be satisfied with the unhappiness and discontentment of Dissatisfaction again. This begins the Search phase of the Powerful Changes Process during which a person begins to scan the horizon looking for a path that will lead to a fulfilling life.

Once a person has embarked upon a Search for this path, fear often starts to creep up. Why fear? Because the person who enters into the Search process looking for something different is stepping into unknown territory.

Several fears come together at this point in the Powerful Changes Process that have the potential to derail the entire process. People begin to fear the unknown. These seekers have experienced levels of their own discomfort in life up to this point, but at least that discomfort is a familiar feeling. When people embark upon a Search without really knowing what exactly they are looking for, the thought that that they might never find what they are after can begin to grip their lives with fear. The fear of the unknown often keeps people from developing or growing as individuals. Even though the known (their current position in life) might be incredibly uncomfortable, for some people the fear of the unknown often keeps them stuck in their discomfort.

For this reason, it is not uncommon during this phase of the Powerful Changes Process for a person to start to backtrack on what appeared to be firm decisions. For instance, when some people experience a Trigger Event that compels them to move out of an unacceptable situation, the fear associated with the Search phase of the Powerful Changes Process will often try to convince them that their previous situations really weren't all that unacceptable!

Beyond a fear of the unknown, some people who are pressing on through the Search phase of the Powerful Changes Process often deal with a fear of failure. As Bryan listened to John Burley's Boot Camp staff members tell their change stories, they often described their Searches at times in terms of desperation or even near panic. The idea that they might never find a way to achieve what they believed to be possible gripped many of these successful people with a fear that their entire lives would be characterized by failure. Fear of the unknown and fear of failure are two common obstacles that need to be addressed before a person can move to the next phase of the Powerful Changes Process.

The important thing to remember during the Search step of a life change is that the most important elements of this step are solidifying a commitment to change and doing the important inner work to determine what you really want out of life. A Search is a time of discovery, not necessarily a time of decision. Discovery begins with figuring out what you want out of life, then beginning the process of finding a path that will lead to what you really want. If people become so gripped by fear that they forget that change is a process that happens over time and not necessarily in an instant, they could become stuck in the status quo indefinitely.

Being afraid that things aren't going to work out, and that you will never find the happiness and peace you crave can often be exaggerated in one's mind during the Search phase. This comes from being in uncharted territory. This fear is to be expected. The fact of the matter is that this fear is healthy, because it motivates people to move forward rather than linger in this uncomfortable phase of the Powerful Changes Process.

Once the Search is over, and a door is discovered that leads to a better life, this fear is replaced by sweet relief! For that reason, Discovering the Door is the fourth step in the Powerful Changes Process and the subject of the next chapter.

Actions Steps

Before you move on to the next chapter, take a moment to go through these action steps.

The Search step in the Powerful Changes Process involves exploration. Since you have already begun to paint a picture of the life that you want to live (see Action Steps at the end of Chapter 2), take some time to go through these exercises to continue to add details to that picture.

1. A big part of the Search phase of the Powerful Changes Process is getting in touch with what you truly want out of life. Take some time to paint a word picture of the kind of life

that you really want to live. To do this, take a piece of paper and sit down in a quiet spot. Write out a schedule for what a typical day of your life might look like, if you were living your ideal life. What would you do each morning? Each afternoon? Each evening? Take some time to paint your mental picture by fantasizing about a typical day in your ideal life.

2. Take some time now to plot your Search strategy. Since the Search step is a process of exploration, think about what you will do in order to explore your options. Books, tape sets, training events, conversations with experts, and conversations with successful friends who you look up to are some of the ways to figure out what direction you should take in life. So, at this point make a commitment to find at least three books that you are going to read as you Search for the path that will lead you to your ideal life.

3. Now make a list of the five people you would most like to talk to about the direction of your life. These can be people you know who are living a life that resembles your ideal life. These could also people you do not know, but would like to spend some time with interviewing them about the road they walked in pursuit of their dreams. What questions would you most like to ask these people? Write those questions down.

4. Now make a list of three tape sets or training events that you would like to listen to or attend as you continue your Search process? If you don't know titles of tape sets or training events, at least write down what areas you would like to investigate in this manner.

5. You should now have a list of books, names, and tape sets or training events that can serve as a starting point for your Search process. Take a moment at this point to put together some action steps around these lists.

  • Write down dates next to the books you have chosen that will give you an idea of when you would like to have the books read.

  • Set up some appointments with the people you listed as men and women you would like to talk to. Make contact with them. Even try to make contact with the famous people you might have listed. You never know, these people might just give you some time. At least make an effort to get in touch with the people that you would most like to talk to. There is a good chance that they are more accessible than you might think.

- Find a tape set that meets the criteria you spelled out in Action Step 4. Make an effort to get your hands on it so you can gain the knowledge it offers. You never know, you might just stumble upon the path to a better life that you have been searching for. (See the end of this book for a list of tape sets by John Burley and Bryan Fergus).

- Finally, investigate training events that could potentially steer you in the right direction. If you are interested in investigating wealth-creating strategies, feel free to visit www.johnburley.com for a schedule of John's training events. If you are interested in self-improvement or spiritual development review the list of books and tapes recommended by John Burley and Bryan Fergus at the end of this book.

The important thing to remember is that the Search phase in the Powerful Changes Process is all about exploration and discovery. Give yourself the freedom to explore. Remember that fear is a common and natural emotional experience that many people face during the Search process. Your fears during the Search phase of the Powerful Changes Process are nothing more than indicators that you need to keep moving forward. Resist the urge to move backwards in the Powerful Changes Process. After all, the last thing you really want to let happen in your life is to settle for a nagging sense of perpetual Dissatisfaction. Persevere in the Search phase of your process and before you know it, you too will Discover the Door that leads to the life you are craving and so rightly deserve!

Chapter 5

Knock And It Will Open!

The Lady or The Tiger?

In Frank Stockton's classic short story entitled *The Lady or the Tiger*, Stockton tells the story of a fictitious king in a barbaric land who always allowed chance and fate to determine the destiny of accused criminals. In this King's land, if a subject of the king was accused of a crime, the king would assemble his people in a large arena where they would all witness the judgment passed on the accused criminal. The passing of judgment was always associated with pomp and circumstance, but the element that filled these occasions with suspense was the method that the king used to determine someone's fate.

The king would sit high on a platform on one side of the arena. The accused criminal would then be led out into the arena through a large door. The subjects of the king would murmur with anticipation and suspense as the subject faced a pair of doors in the wall of the arena.

Both of the doors were identical, but behind each door awaited a drastically different fate. Behind one door was a beautiful maiden. If the accused subject chose that door, not only were the charges against him dismissed, he was also given the maiden as a wife. In fact, the king would bless their wedding on the spot. A priest, a choir, and dancers would be released into the arena to officiate the lucky couple's marriage ceremony. Behind the other door awaited a ferocious tiger. The tiger would be denied food for days before the judgment was passed in the arena. If the accused subject opened the door that led to the tiger, the tiger would pounce, the crowd would shriek in terror, and the accused subject's fate would be sealed with his own death.

Trial days were popular in the kingdom. People would come from all over to witness a possible wedding or a possible mauling. Nobody knew what to expect – not even the king and of course not even the accused subject. When it came time to choose his fate, the subject approached the two doors and had a very important decision to make. The odds were even. He had a 50/50 chance of opening either door to discover either his new bride or his own death. Nothing on the doors indicated which option was hidden behind each door. The outcome of the day for the accused person was simply a matter of chance. When the accused man opened the door that he had chosen what would he find – the lady or the tiger?

There are times in life when many feel as though they are in that poor accused subject's position. We stand at a crossroads in life with what seems like two figurative doors in front of us with a choice to make. Options lay out before us. Both options can look like doors that could possibly be opened onto new and exciting adventures in life. At the same time, we fear that opening a particular door might unleash a tiger of frustration and heartache that we might never be able to recover from. The Search phase of the Powerful Changes Process is a lot like being in the barbaric king's arena described in Frank Stockton's story.

During the Search phase of the Powerful Changes Process we open door after door looking for the one that is hiding our path to a better life. Dissatisfaction has made us so uncomfortable that we know something has to change in our lives if we are ever going to experience fulfillment and peace. A Trigger Event makes us angry or frustrated enough so that we do something about the unhappiness of Dissatisfaction. This Trigger Event pushes us to move out of our discomfort zones by making the status quo intolerable. Then we set about searching for a path that will help us realize and experience a better life – an ideal life.

While we move through the Search phase, fear can start to creep in. We wonder if we will ever find what we are looking for. We wonder if we will ever open the right door that will lead us to the fulfillment of our dreams. As we look at one option after another we wonder if there is a way, an avenue, or a path out there that will ever lead to personal fulfillment and even financial freedom. And then finally we find it. We read a book, attend a seminar, have a conversation, watch a television program, read a magazine article, or listen to a radio interview and something finally clicks. In that moment we know that we have found what we have been searching for. To put it simply, we have Discovered the Door that opens onto the better life that we have been craving!

The End of the Search

The fourth phase of the Powerful Changes Process is Discovering the Door. This phase in the Powerful Changes Process is really nothing more than the conclusion of the Search. As a seeker looks for a way to transform his unacceptable situation into a life that brings more joy and peace to his days, he finally finds the path that he knows will help him make that transformation. As a person searches for a life path that will alleviate his pain and ease some of the stress and tension created by Dissatisfaction, inevitably a door is discovered.

During the Search phase of the Powerful Changes Process, a person evaluates all sorts of options. For instance, if a person is searching for a path to financial freedom, he might read a dozen business books or watch a few infomercials that seem to offer a wealth creation strategy that makes sense. He might even buy a video course on making money through classified advertising, but after he gets it home and watches it he comes to the conclusion that it's just not for him. Maybe this seeker then finds a book that convinces him that real estate investing is the way to create the passive income that he knows will lead to his personal financial freedom. At the same time he realizes the book isn't enough. The book just scratches the surface and doesn't really address all of his nagging questions. He needs more information. Maybe he's still not totally convinced that investing in real estate is the path that he should choose to follow in his quest for financial freedom. At the same time, he has a sneaking suspicion that it is. So, he goes to a real estate investing training seminar and learns from experts and talks to people who are already moving toward their financial freedom. At that point his mind is made up. He is convinced that he has Discovered the Door that will lead to his financial freedom.

This short example reveals the heart of Discovering the Door. This step in the Powerful Changes Process is really all about finally finding a strategy or path that will bring about positive changes. Discovering the Door is the point in the change process when a person becomes convinced that he has found a way to fulfill his dreams. Discovering the Door can take many forms. It can be as simple as signing up for a seminar or deciding to go back to school to cross train for a new career. Discovering the Door can take the form of developing a new friendship or becoming part of a networking group. It can even take the form of finding a path that leads to financial freedom.

Discovering The Door To Financial Prosperity

For many of the members of John Burley's Boot Camp staff and the students who attend his Boot Camp, the door they discovered was a book that has changed thousand's of lives. John Burley's book entitled *Money Secrets of the Rich* is a virtual encyclopedia of sensible financial strategies that people can use to establish their financial health. In the pages of *Money Secrets of the Rich*, John defines the money habits that cause people to become wealthy and financially free. It's a "How To" book that walks people through a series of action steps that have the potential to turn them into millionaires while becoming completely debt-free in very a short period of time. This international best-selling book has served as a door that people have discovered in the process of searching for their personal financial freedom. Once they find it, read it, and put some of its strategies into practice, people report that they are wealthier and even more content in life. The strength of *Money Secrets of the Rich* is that the information contained in its pages has the power to totally transform a person's financial position in life. If the advice spelled out in *Money Secrets of the Rich* is followed, a financial disaster can be transformed into a flourishing future.

The truth is that financial problems are a chief source of frustration and stress in the Free World. People make bad money decisions that bog them down in consumer debt and rob them of the money they work so hard to get. The fact is that financial pressures are a leading cause of divorce and even many of the stress-related illnesses that rob people of a good quality of life.

When people paint the picture of what their perfect life looks like, that picture usually includes a positive change in their financial position. Unfortunately, many people don't know how to take the little steps that will lead to a huge leap in their financial health.

The problem with most financial books is that they stop short of spelling out how to take the right steps that will lead to financial abundance. Fortunately, John Burley didn't go down that path. When John wrote *Money Secrets of the Rich* he went to great lengths to include a step-by-step plan of action that anyone can follow. In fact, John tested all of his action steps by asking a freshman in high school that he knows to perform them. He wanted to make sure that the steps were easy to follow. When John teaches or writes, his chief concern is the success of his readers and his students. Rather than spouting theory, John wanted to put in place practical tools in the tool chest of every one of his readers so that they could experience financial freedom for themselves. That's why John wrote *Money Secrets of the Rich*.

Many of the people who have become members of John Burley's Advanced Investing Boot Camps Discovered the Door to the better life that they were looking for when they picked up and read *Money Secrets of the Rich*. It has been an important tool that has led to a better financial life for thousands upon thousands of people. It's a great example of what a door to a better life actually looks like.

A door can even take the form of attending a seminar, listening to a tape set or any of the other options that people pursue as they search for an option that will help them fulfill their dreams. As Bryan interviewed John Burley's Advanced Investing Boot Camp Staff members at length to discover their Powerful Changes stories, it was clear that as they envisioned their ideal lives they were all looking for an avenue that included boosting their financial health so that they could have the freedom to spend their time and energy on the things that they most wanted out of life. The door they discovered was an investment strategy that enabled them to shed their Dissatisfaction and step into the freedom of a life anchored in security and ultimately joy. Let's take a moment to look at a few of their discovery stories to get a firmer grasp of what this step in the Powerful Changes Process really looks like.

For a FREE 25 Page Report on

"The Seven Levels of Investor"

Visit www.johnburley.com.

Adrian Oakman's Discovery Story

Since we've been tracking Adrian Oakman's story through the steps of the Powerful Changes Process thus far, let's take a moment to look at his discovery story. As Adrian, a dairy farmer who wanted to spend more time with his family, came to terms with the Dissatisfaction that characterized his life, he realized that something needed to change. Adrian's dramatic Trigger Event story pushed him to begin a Search for a better life. When Adrian embarked upon his Search for a life of freedom and joy, John Burley had not yet published *Money Secrets of the Rich*. John had produced several tape sets that explained the step-by-step basics of his real estate investing strategies. Adrian realized that investing in real estate would generate passive income for his family.

Since Adrian was looking for a way to spend less of his time working and more of his time with his family, he decided to focus his Search on the possibility of replacing his farming income with a passive income produced by a variety of real estate investments. At the same time, Adrian wasn't certain that he could actually pull off the switch from being a farmer to becoming an adept property investor. He needed to investigate this life path further. So Adrian decided that he needed to see if what John Burley had said on the tape set he had invested in was actually true.

At that point in the Search phase of his Powerful Changes Process, Adrian made a bold move. He placed a phone call to John Burley's office. Throughout the course of that conversation Adrian discovered that John Burley was no "snake oil" salesman. Adrian discovered that unlike many real estate investing trainers, John himself is actively involved in investing in real estate on a regular basis. John actually acquires hundreds of investment properties a year. This information caused Adrian to believe that John's strategies would work. However, Adrian still needed a little more convincing.

Adrian's moment of discovery came when he attended John Burley's Advanced Investing Boot Camp. He traveled from a small town in New Zealand to the bustling metropolis of Phoenix, Arizona. Phoenix is the sixth largest city in the United States of America. It's quite a bit different from the lush green fields of New Zealand. Adrian felt out of his element as he stepped into the training room on his first day as a Boot Camp student. However, when John began introducing his staff members – real people who had implemented John's strategies and discovered their path to financial abundance – Adrian knew that he had Discovered the Door that would lead his family to the better life that they all deserved. As he flew home to New Zealand, Adrian knew that his life would never be the same. His discontentment had been replaced by relief.

Joe Arlt's Discovery Story

You have already been introduced to Joe Arlt in the pages of this book. Joe was the business school graduate who was the envy of his peers. He's the one who had the prestigious job with a reputable company that flew him all over the globe as a representative of the corporation. Joe's story of Dissatisfaction is spelled out in Chapter 2. Take a moment and reacquaint yourself with it if you need to.

All of the relentless travel and inner unhappiness caused Joe to become dissatisfied with his life. He knew that something needed to change in his life if he was ever going to enjoy his days on Planet Earth. Even though Joe was admired and respected by his employers and his professional peers, he couldn't imagine spending the rest of his life struggling to climb up the ladder of corporate America. The politics and posturing associated with moving up the corporate food chain can be tiring. Joe was tired. He knew he needed to find a new way to achieve his financial freedom that wouldn't continuously rob his life of joy and peace.

Joe Arlt was already familiar with the positive potential that investing in real estate could bring to his situation. Joe's mother had been a successful realtor and had invested in real estate personally for years. At the same time, Joe had no interest in being a landlord. He began searching for a path that would take the best that investing in real estate had to offer without requiring him to fit into a mold that he wasn't interested in. That's when Joe found John Burley.

Joe's discovery story is notoriously well known among John Burley's circle of friends. Joe's Search ended when he attended a real estate investing training event that featured John Burley as its keynote speaker. Joe's background in corporate America had thoroughly shaped the way he viewed business opportunities. His naturally analytical mind, formal education and his vast experience caused him to be skeptical as he stepped into this real estate training event. At the same time, Joe's skepticism collided with his internal hope that real estate investing might be the path to the better life that he was looking for. He was skeptical that he had found the door that would open onto his ideal life. At the same time, Joe was genuinely hoping that this seminar would indeed show him that investing in real estate was that door. His internal dissonance raised Joe's stress and anxiety levels. Still, he stepped into the training determined to fully engage in the experience.

At the same time, Joe had another "obstacle" to overcome. His fantastic education from one of the world's most prestigious business schools had completely colored his perspective of how business works in the real world. While education is a wonderful thing that should be treasured by everyone fortunate enough to receive it, achieving a degree can also give people the false sense that they know everything there is to know in their field of expertise. The best educational experiences turn students into lifelong learners who are passionate about discovering the truth even long after they have received their degrees. The idea that a four year degree or even an eight year degree can give people all of the tools that they will ever need for success in the real world is simply wishful thinking. We live in a culture of change. There are always new things to know and new ways to look at old problems. When Joe stepped into the real estate seminar that he had signed up for, his education caused him to question and even doubt much of what he heard that day.

Today, Joe Arlt and John Burley are very close personal friends. Beyond that, they have become business partners and are both at the helm of a national real estate investing program that is making a lot of people a lot of money. They often joke around about the day they first met each other. John was at the front of the room laying out the simple steps that people could follow in order to use real estate as a source for passive income. John was even spelling out a strategy that could allow a person to be an active real estate investor without getting bogged down in land lording. John was presenting his material in his usual manner. He was laying out a simple step-by step system that the average person could easily follow with little difficulty. As Joe listened he began raising his hand with question after question. He challenged most of what John was saying to the point that he became something of a nuisance to the rest of the people in the class.

Today, John and Joe joke about that fateful day as they both enjoy a life of financial freedom and personal fulfillment. To date, Joe Arlt has been involved in more than five hundred real estate transactions. He uses the wrap or cash flow strategy that John taught the day Joe attended his seminar. And again, John and Joe are business partners who have turned the world of real estate investing upside down with their innovative strategies and assertive ambitions. At the same time, they are both committed to making this world a better place to live for as many people as possible.

Joe Discovered a Door that opened onto the better life that he had been looking for for so long. What Joe also discovered was that the life he found was better than he had ever imagined. Beyond volunteering as one of John Burley's Advanced Investing Boot Camp staff members, Joe now teaches other people how to follow the path that he has been walking now for years.

Sweet Relief

Like all of the steps or phases of the Powerful Changes Process, the Discovering the Door step carries its own set of emotions. As a quick review, let's take another look at the emotions that surround the other phases of the Powerful Changes Process. The

Dissatisfaction phase of the Powerful Changes Process is characterized by a strong inner sense of unhappiness. The unhappiness of Dissatisfaction builds until a Trigger Event turns that unhappiness into anger. The Trigger Event phase, which could be more accurately called a Trigger Event "moment", is the point at which a person gets angry enough to do something about this inner sense or unhappiness or discontentment. The next step in the Powerful Changes Process, the Search phase is often characterized by fear. As a people get pushed out of their discomfort zones, they step into uncharted territory and often experience the fear of the unknown. As the Search for a better life continues, seekers often experience another fear – the fear of failure. The thought that they might never be able to find a path that leads to a better life causes a certain sense of panic to begin to creep into their minds. So the first three phases of the Powerful Changes Process are characterized by unhappiness, anger, and fear.

All of these emotions have a negative connotation. Nobody likes to be unhappy, angry or afraid. That is why the emotion connected to Discovering the Door is so welcomed as a part of the Powerful Changes Process. The chief emotion connected to Discovering the Door is relief. All of the negative emotions of unhappiness, anger and fear are transformed into feelings of excitement, anticipation, and hope. These feelings all combine to fill someone who has Discovered the Door to a better life with a sense of true relief.

This relief comes from the realization that a person has finally found the thing that he or she has been looking for and working toward. The long Search is over, the fear starts to diminish, and the adrenaline rush of struggling for survival starts to fade. What sets in to replace the inner swirl of unhappiness, anger, and fear is the sense of a new beginning or a new lease on life. As the people in this book Discovered the Door that opened onto the path to a better life, they all reported experiencing a calming sense of relief.

It might be that you are in the midst of a life change. Maybe you have picked up this book hoping that it will give you some answers. Chances are pretty good that if you are reading this book looking for a path to a better life, you are probably in the Search phase of your Powerful Changes Process. Your inner life might be a swirl of unhappiness, anger, and even fear. While those are very uncomfortable emotions to experience, take some encouragement from knowing that relief is just around the corner. The wonderful thing about relief is that it frees people up to take bold action. In fact, Taking Action is the next phase of the Powerful Changes Process. More on that in the next chapter.

Action Steps

Before you move on to the next chapter, take a moment to go through these action steps.

Discovering the Door that will open onto your better life is simply culmination of the Search process. In the last chapter, you were encouraged to formulate a plan for your Search. You made a list of books, conversations, tape sets, and even training events that you were going to expose yourself to. The action steps in this chapter are going to assume that you are implementing your Search plan. By the way, if you're not, go back and do the actions steps for Chapter 4 NOW! If you truly want to make progress in your quest for a more centered, less frazzled, and nearly ideal life, then it is essential that you work through the actions steps spelled out at the end of each chapter. With that said, the action steps in this chapter are going to focus on knowing when you have Discovered your Door.

It's one thing to long for a path that will lead you to a better life. It is quite another thing to know when you have actually found that door. The people interviewed in connection with this book all knew that the door they were looking for would include a way for them to generate passive income so that they could spend less time working hard and more time focusing on the things that they really wanted out of life. So, when they found John Burley's real estate investing strategies they knew they had Discovered the Door they were looking for. John's strategies offered them a way to generate the quick cash to handle any past or current financial needs and then the long-term passive income that would provide them with a lifetime of financial freedom. So, these people knew they had Discovered the Door they were looking for because they had already thought about what that door might look like.

There's an old adage that says, "If you aim at nothing, you will hit it every time". In other words, if you don't really know what you are looking for, chances are pretty good you will never find it. So, take a moment and complete the following action steps so you will have an idea of what type of door you are looking for as you go about your Search.

1. Which area of your life would you most like to bring changes to? Your professional life? Your family life? Your financial life? Your spiritual life? As you move through the change process it is important to have some idea of what part of your life is causing you the most Dissatisfaction so that you can Search for a solution to that problem.

2. With that area of your life in mind, what would you truly like to see happen in that part of your life? If you are looking to transform your professional life, would you like to find a job that would allow you to take more control of projects? If you are looking to bring changes to your family life, would you like to find a way to spend more time focusing on your primary relationships? If you are looking to change your financial life, would you like to find a way to get out of debt quickly or get a better return on your investments? If you are looking to transform your spiritual life, would you like to find a way to be more centered and filled with purpose and meaning? Take a moment to reflect on these thoughts.

3. Now that you have gotten in touch with what you are truly looking for in life, you are better prepared to Discover your Door. If you are looking to transform your financial life by getting out of debt, your door will include a debt reduction plan that you can live with. Write a definitive statement that includes an important element that will characterize the door you are looking for. In fact, use this formula: Because I want _____ in my life, my door will include _____.

Discovering the Door is an amazing experience. Once you have an idea of the kind of changes that you want to see happen in your life, you open yourself up to Discovering the Door that opens onto the life that you have dreamed of living. Having an idea of the kind of changes that you are after will allow you to Discover the Door you are looking for without having to blindly stumble from one possibility to the next. But once you Discover the Door you have been searching for, the next step in the

Powerful Changes Process is where the real progress starts to happen. Let's turn our attention to the next phase of the your change process now – Taking Action.

Chapter 6

Time To Take Off!

Burning Ships

Hernan Cortez was one of the most adventurous and accomplished explorers that ever set sail from the shores of Spain. His methods were unconventional. In fact, he was often cruel in his approach to the new cultures that he and his men encountered when they set foot on the shores of the New World. And yet, Cortez was exceptionally courageous and singularly committed to exploring this New World on behalf of the Spanish throne. Cortez traveled west looking to establish a foothold in the New World for his Mother Country. Beyond that, Cortez wanted to find wealth and resources for himself and his countrymen.

Along the way, Cortez was keenly aware that his explorations would mean great rewards from the rulers of Spain upon his return. Cortez had discovered a way to help his country, fill his own personal coffers, and garner the fame that he was desperately seeking when he left friends and family behind to explore the New World. He was looking to discover new lands, vast riches, and the respect and admiration of the Spanish nobles. When Cortez left the shores of Spain and arrived on the eastern coast of Mexico, a lot was riding on his exploration. The stakes were high and success was imperative. Spain had invested a lot of money in Cortez' exploratory journey. He had to succeed. Failure was not an option. Turning back was out of the question.

So when Cortez' men started to grumble about heading home,

Hernan Cortez became concerned. His men had landed on the eastern shore of Mexico. They had established a beachhead, built a make shift fortress, and finished their jobs – or so they thought. It is clear from the historical record that many of Cortez' men did not expect to be gone from home as long as they were. When it became apparent that there journey to the New World was going to keep them away from their motherland for years instead of months, many of the men started to seriously consider the possibility of taking matters into their own hands.

Cortez' men were also upset because of the unreasonable demands that he placed upon them. Cortez worked his men hard. He pushed them to the breaking point of physical and emotional exhaustion. Historians speculate that because Cortez himself was an immensely driven man, he had no qualms when it came to demanding that his men drive themselves beyond their own resources. The prospect of staying away from home for too long and the harsh working and living conditions combined to push Cortez' men to their breaking points.

Word came to Cortez that some of his men were beginning to talk about mutiny. They had devised an ill-conceived plan to row the landing boats out to Cortez' ships that were anchored out further in the bay. They were then going to pull up the anchors, hoist the sails, and set sail for home. In essence, they were going to steal Cortez' ships and simply go home. Cortez caught wind of their scheme. He had too much riding on his expedition to be thwarted by a group of grumpy mercenaries and soldiers. The stakes were too high for him to allow the men to abandon the mission and head home empty-handed. So in a bold move that still leaves historians gaping with opened mouths to this very day, Cortez took measures that insured that his men would stay committed to the exploration of the New World.

One day, Cortez gathered all of his men along the shore. He addressed the issues that his men were facing. He told them that he was aware that some of them had mutinous intentions. He directed his men to look out across the bay at his ships anchored in the calm waters. Then Cortez gave the signal, and the men positioned on landing boats near his grand ships carried out his orders. Simultaneously, Cortez' loyal men set fire to all of his ships. The men on the shore must have gasped as they watched their only link to home and their old way of life go up in flames and sink to the bottom of the bay. Turning back was no longer an option. Abandoning the mission to explore the New World was out of the question. In one bold action, Cortez sunk his ships and made it impossible for his men to return prematurely to the life they had once known.

Taking Bold Action

The story of Cortez burning his ships to insure that his men would stay committed to the task ahead is a legendary story that inspires and amazes people to this day. It is also a marvelous illustration of the need to take bold action in order to make real progress in life. That's why this story is the perfect way to open this chapter on the fifth step of the Powerful Changes Process. The fifth step of the Powerful Changes Process is Taking Action. While all of the steps or phases of the change process are important, this one is where the rubber meets the road, so to speak. In this fifth step of the Powerful Changes Process, a person commits to taking the necessary steps to transform the unacceptable situation that is currently filling life with so much inner dissatisfaction.

Once people have come to terms with their inner Dissatisfaction and experienced a Trigger Event that makes living with the status quo impossible, the Search for something better begins. Once that Search results in Discovering a Door that opens onto a path to a better life, it is time to start taking steps along that path. In short, it's time to Take Action on what the Search uncovered as the way to transform an unfulfilled life into a life of peace and meaning. It's time to burn some ships and fully commit to following a new path in life.

That's the key to the fifth step of the Powerful Changes Process. In this step, people get down to doing what needs to be done to transform their inner Dissatisfaction into a future filled with possibilities and hope. During the Taking Action phase of the Powerful Changes Process, people take the first steps in a definitive plan of action that will lead to a life altering change. This phase of the Powerful Changes Process is so important because it represents the full commitment of a person to move toward a changed life. When people Discover the Door during the fourth step in the Powerful Changes Process, they become convinced that they have found a path that will lead them to the life that they have been looking for. But simply Discovering a Door isn't enough. That door has to be opened and walked through in order for real progress to happen toward the pursuit of a better life. Once people begin to take definitive steps in a plan of action, they demonstrate to themselves and the people in their lives that they truly intend to lead a different lifestyle from that moment on.

Getting Bogged Down In The Change Process

Unfortunately many people get bogged down or stuck at this step in the Powerful Changes Process. After having experienced Dissatisfaction and a major Trigger Event, a personal Search has led to the Discovery of a Door that could be walked through in order to move toward a promising new way of life. But sometimes personal doubts start to creep back into the mix at this point. A person can know what needs to be done and even how to do it, but sometimes something deeply programmed into a person's inner life can cause him or her to become paralyzed in the Powerful Changes Process before action is ever taken. It could be that fear of failure that kept popping up during the Search phase of the process. The fear of failure often rears its ugly head when a person is trying to make significant changes in life.

Surprisingly enough, the fear of success can be just as debilitating. Let's say a person is truly interested in becoming financially independent. He is smart enough to realize that simply working harder at a nine-to-five job won't necessarily get him there. So he begins to look for new ways to create wealth. His investigation shows him that the vast majority of wealthy people who have ever lived on this planet got wealthy because they were able to acquire assets that passively generated positive cash flow. He looks at investing in the stock market and even real estate. He's convinced that he can create a passive income by buying properties and leasing them out to occupants who are willing to pay a good monthly rate.

But then something happens to him on the inside. He begins to remember everything that he ever learned about "rich" people from his middle class upbringing. His parents, grandparents, religious teachers, and even some of his teachers in school convinced him that rich people are suspect. He was taught that in order for rich

CHAPTER 6

people to get ahead, most of them had to step on middle class
people, cheat, and steal in order to claw their way to the top.

So now, this person is convinced that he has the knowledge he
needs to become independently wealthy. He is convinced that he
even has the abilities and skills that it will take to create passive
income for his family. However, the fear of how he will perceived if
he becomes "rich" stops him dead in his tracks. He's afraid that if
he achieves the lifestyle that he wants, his parents or religious
leaders or even close friends will turn their backs on him. In a very
real way, he's afraid of his own potential for financial success.

The pressure to conform to the status quo can be paralyzing. If
a person has a spouse who is adverse to change or if so-called
friends are unsympathetic to a person's inner dissatisfaction, he
might be prevented from ever taking positive action and achieving
positive change.

Unfortunately, if people fail to Take Action at this point in the
Powerful Changes Process, the effects can be devastating. Here's
why. If after getting a glimpse of the possibility of a better life
people force themselves to go back to their old ingrained habits and
patterns, the feelings of Dissatisfaction that were felt during the
first phase of the Powerful Changes Process can become
exaggerated and more intense than ever. If people feel that their
situations in life are never going to allow them to pursue the better
life that they know is out there, then Dissatisfaction can turn to
despair and depression and a life that will be filled with regrets.

The human mind is an amazing thing. It can open us up to all
of the possibilities of a potentially better life. At the same time, it
can keep us from reaching out and laying hold of that better life for
a variety of reasons. The important thing to remember during the
Taking Action phase of the change process is to PRESS ON! TAKE
ACTION! The only way to answer critics is by proving them wrong
with a lifestyle that benefits the human community and fills a life
with meaning and fulfillment.

Those first steps toward a better life can often be the scariest
and the most exciting at the same time. The people around a
person moving toward the fulfillment of his or her dreams don't
often understand or even support steps toward self-improvement.
At this point it is important to remember that those people don't
have to deal with the inner dissatisfaction that the person seeking

change has struggled with for so long. Fortunately, many people ignore their critics and Take Action. That's exactly what John Burley did many years ago. Let's take a look at his story and the story of some others who have taken action and moved toward the fulfillment of their dreams.

John Burley's Action Story

Only two people really supported John Burley when he decided to quit his lucrative financial planning practice and step into the world of being a full-time active real estate investor. John's soon-to-be wife, Shari, and his father, Bob, believed in John enough to know that he could make it in the unconventional world of professional investing. John had been raised to believe that the best thing a man could do with his life was to get a good white collar job, climb the corporate ladder, and gain partial ownership of a money making company. John had spent quite a bit of time climbing this ladder. His bosses loved him. He out-produced most of the people in his company. John made a lot of money for a lot of people, including himself.

However, after playing the game by the corporate world's rules for years, John stepped away from high-rise office buildings and suits and ties on a daily basis and established his own financial planning company. John started making good money in his own practice right away. He knew the ins and outs of the financial planning world so well that he quickly had a word-of-mouth following that resulted in a backlog of potential clients who all wanted to benefit from his financial prowess. John focused on the pick of the litter. He spent his time and energy working with the wealthiest and most successful clients who came to him. However, along the way John learned something about himself and the financial planning industry.

John quickly discovered that the way to get ahead in the financial planning industry was to sell clients investment products that paid the financial planner the best commissions. In other words, John discovered that a large number of financial planners were more concerned about producing large commissions for themselves than they were with truly looking out for the best interests of their clients. That's what John discovered about the financial planning industry. The thing that John discovered about *himself* in this whole process is that his personal integrity is more important to him than any amount of money. As John met with client after client he found himself focusing on the client's needs and setting his own financial prosperity on the back burner. This didn't sit well with the companies whose investment products John regularly sold. On top of that, John began to grow weary of meeting with clients everyday at the cost of spending his time doing the things he most wanted to do. All of these factors combined to make John realize that his future didn't lie in financial planning. He wanted more out of life. He started to investigate the possibility of making a living through actively investing in real estate. John had been aware of the potential of real estate to create passive income for some time. In fact, he had even ventured into the world of real estate investing on occasion. A deal here and there had made John some nice chunks of cash over the years, but up to this point he had never really considered investing in real estate on a full-time basis.

That all changed when John stumbled upon a training course that helped him to see that investing in real estate was the path that would lead him to fulfill his dream of a happier and more settled life. Although that course served as a springboard for John, he quickly realized that there were many holes in the education that he had been given that still needed to be filled. From that point on, John began a lifelong active study of real estate investing. The result was that John eventually went on to pioneer innovative real estate techniques that this first training never even mentioned.

When John decided to close his financial planning practice and move from northern California to Phoenix, Arizona to invest in real estate full time, most of the people in his life thought he was crazy. Why would a young man with a financially prosperous business, a flashy big Mercedes Benz, and a beautiful girlfriend sell everything off and move to the desert to begin buying and selling houses for a living? When John burned his ships and began to invest his time, energy, and money in average single-family homes, the real estate market was struggling in the Phoenix area. Yet John believed that Phoenix was the perfect place for what he wanted to do and that the timing for getting started was perfect.

Of course, time has proven John right. Today he has a real estate portfolio that includes interest in over one thousand properties internationally. Not only that, John's theories, systems, and strategies have made thousands of people financially free and abundant. Fortunately for John, he had the ability, knowledge and ambition to take bold action to move toward the life he always wanted. The support of Shari and his father, Bob, provided added support that only served to bolster his confidence to burn his ships and Take Action.

John McCants' Action Story

John McCants is one of the nicest people on the planet. He has a generous heart, a winning smile, and a calm assurance that puts the people around him at ease. On top of all of these winning qualities, John McCants has a desire to help people, especially the people closest to him. As destiny would have it, John McCants and John Burley became very good friends through a chance meeting. John McCants and John Burley happened to attend the training seminar that moved John Burley to pursue real estate investing full-time together. Since then, John Burley and John McCants have developed a brother-like relationship. They vacation together, work together, and each considers the other to be a valued and trusted confidant.

Both John Burley and John McCants will tell you that one of the keys to their success as real estate investors is having close friendships with people who have pushed them to excel rather than grow stagnant. John McCants and John Burley have filled that role for one another and other for many years. As a result, they have both become better at what they do. They have both achieved a great deal of success as professional investors. In fact, John McCants is one of the featured speakers at John Burley's training events. He has carved a niche in the northwest region of the United Sates as a cutting edge investor who specializes in purchasing properties through courthouse auctions and foreclosures.

However, John McCants wasn't always the happy, centered, and successful man that he is today. Before achieving his personal success and finding the freedom to use his time and energy as he pleased, John McCants had made a very good living for more than a dozen years in the insurance industry. Prior to attending a real estate investing seminar, John McCants had been a model employee in the insurance department of a local mortgage banker. He worked hard, made a good living, and kept his bosses happy. At the same time, John McCants just wasn't as happy as he thought he should be. He simply wasn't satisfied with his life.

Some people need to feel passionate about what they are doing in order to be content. Some people need to know that the way they spend their hours on a daily basis has some sense of purpose to it. John McCants is one of those people. He's not satisfied to move through life in a nine-to-five existence working hard for a few weeks of vacation every year. He wants to spend his days pursuing a greater purpose.

A growing sense of Dissatisfaction and frustration over his unfulfilling life kept John McCants from really enjoying his days. This growing sense of discontentment pushed him to respond to a Trigger Event experience in his life. Like all of the successful people interviewed for Powerful Changes, John McCants began a Search for something better that led him to the same real estate investing training that John Burley attended as a student. They struck up a friendship as fellow students treading into new waters. Like John Burley, John McCants became convinced that the financial freedom he was looking for could be found by pursuing an investment portfolio of real estate that created a passive monthly income. John McCants didn't intend to use this investment portfolio to simply sit back and retire into nothingness. He simply wanted to be the captain of his own destiny and the one steering the ship of his life. Most people give that control over to someone else. John McCants wasn't content to do that.

When John McCants went home from his introductory real estate training event, his head was full of possibilities. He knew that he could make it as an active investor. He was confident that he had the skills and abilities to get something started that would lead him to personal freedom and the better life he was looking for. He got back home after a weekend that inspired him to take action on what he had learned. He had made it through the Dissatisfaction step of the Powerful Changes Process. He had taken his Trigger Event seriously. His Search had led him to Discover the Door that opened onto a path that would help him achieve his financial goals. The next thing to do was to simply Take Action.

A simple thought gripped John McCants as he traveled to his office the following Monday morning. He knew that he could never be satisfied with the status quo again. Staying the same had simply become more painful than making the necessary changes to fulfill his personal dreams. Taking Action in the Powerful Changes Process is all about making a complete commitment to making positive changes. The action step that John McCants took that morning demonstrated to himself and the people around him that he was going to live a different life from that moment onward.

As John McCants arrived at his office building that morning, he stepped into the elevator and pushed the button to travel to the floor that was the home to the corporation he worked for. The elevator stopped at the floor, the doors opened, and John McCants looked out onto the same four walls that had been his professional home for the past several years. Something in John McCants immediately connected everything that he had discovered and come to realize in a single moment. He froze. He couldn't step out of the elevator into his office. Somehow he knew that taking those steps would be steps taken backwards. Something told him that if he didn't boldly Take Action right there and then, he would most likely slip right back into his old habits and patterns and experience the same old Dissatisfaction that had been nagging at him for so long.

While John McCants stood there and considered all of this truth, the elevator doors closed and the elevator carried him back to the lobby of the building. He stepped out of the elevator and back into the lobby to collect his head for a few moments. Coworkers passed him. The same familiar faces that he had seen every day of his life for years surrounded him. Everything around John McCants was the same, and yet internally he wanted everything in his life to be different. At that moment, John McCants knew exactly what he had to do. He had to Take

Action. So he stepped back into the elevator, and rode it back up to the floor that housed his office. Once there, John McCants walked through the hallways that had been his familiar haunt for so long. He smiled at his coworkers, while walking determinedly to his boss' office. At that point, John stepped into his boss' office, explained to him what he was experiencing inside, and gave his notice. To put it simply, John McCants quit his job. Twenty minutes later, office security walked him out of the building and the rest, as they say is history!

John McCants' bold action step was the step he needed to take. At the same time, quitting a job isn't necessarily an action step that everyone needs to take. We're not even remotely recommending that you personally go out today and quit your job. However, in John McCants case, stepping away from his job was the action step that allowed him to move forward in the Powerful Changes Process.

Such a bold action step might seem careless and even naïve to some people. But the fact of the matter is that John McCants knew that he needed to boldly Take Action in order to fully commit himself to moving out of his unacceptable situation into a better life. He knew that he had what it took to fulfill his dreams. His Search had led him to Discover the Door. He was certain that he could implement the simple strategies that would allow him to excel as an active investor. The only thing left to do was act. So John McCants did. He quit his job.

After that he began to commit his time and energy to working his plan to become a successful investor. John McCants plan has been refined over the years, but his basic strategy has stayed the same. It worked. His bold action moved him in the right direction.

Today John McCants is a centered man. He is spiritually aware, financially free, and professionally respected as a mentor to young entrepreneurs who are striving to make their own marks in the investing world. John is a savvy and successful investor in the northwestern United States. He makes a great living as an active real estate investor and enjoys an abundant and growing passive income. John McCants never would have been able to enjoy the success that he experiences today if he had stepped back into life as usual on that fateful morning. Taking Action doesn't always have to be so bold or even so dramatic, but it does have to happen if a person is serious about making positive changes in life.

The Excitement of Action

Discovering a Door that opens onto a path that leads to a better life fills a person with relief. Dissatisfaction and the unhappiness and discontentment it creates turns to anger during the Trigger Event phase of the Powerful Changes Process. That anger then turns to a low level of fear as a person searches for a way to make the possibility of a better life a concrete reality. Once that Search leads to a Door that opens onto a path that will confidently lead to the fulfillment of personal dreams, fears are transformed into relief. But the emotional dynamics of the Powerful Changes Process don't peak at relief. The just keep getting better!

Once people have Discovered the Door to a better life, Taking Action steps through that Door and onto the path to fulfilling a personal destiny begins to fill people with a growing sense of excitement. Knowing that you are taking steps toward improving your life can be very exciting. Discovering new things and embarking on a new direction in life explode into excitement during the Taking Action phase of the Powerful Changes Process.

As mentioned earlier in this chapter, failing to take positive action steps in the Powerful Changes Process can lead many to a deep sense of despair and even to depression. Imagine the consequences that John McCants would have suffered if he had not Taken Action after Discovering the Door of finding financial freedom through investing in real estate. If John McCants had forced himself to settle back into the status quo, his spirit would have been broken. His inner life would have suffered serious damage. His Dissatisfaction would have spiraled out of control. If kept up for long enough, John McCants' refusal to Take Action would eventually led to a life filled with regrets.

However, the other side of the coin of the despair and regret of inaction is the excitement and passion of bold action. When people push open the door that they are confident leads to a better life and step through it, their sense of discovery and self-confidence creates a contagious feeling of excitement. In fact, it is precisely this level of excitement that creates an amazing synergy whenever John Burley's Advanced Investing Boot Camp staff members get together. Because they are all boldly Taking Action toward the fulfillment of their dreams, their excitement is infectious when they spend time together. In fact, after being together this amazing group of people often experiences a surge of confidence and inspiration to move on to take even bolder action in the pursuit of their dreams.

Action Steps

Before you move on to the next chapter, take a moment to go through these action steps.

Since the Taking Action phase of the Powerful Changes Process is all about making a complete commitment to making positive changes, the action steps in this chapter are especially important. Chances are that you have picked up this book and read this far because you are interested in getting your life more in line with what you wish it would be and know it can be. So far you have taken action steps that have encouraged you to dream about what your perfect life would look like. You have developed a Search strategy that will lead you toward a door that leads to a better life. You have taken some time to think about what area or areas of your life that you want to focus on for positive change. You've even come to terms with a handful of characteristics that will help you recognize that door when you discover it.

Once you have Discovered your Door, it's important that you Take Action. Without Taking Action in your pursuit of better life, your dreams will never become a reality. At this point in your Powerful Changes Process, you might not have Discovered your Door yet. If not, keep Searching. However, chances are pretty good that you have begun to get an idea of the kind of steps that you need to take to bring about positive changes in your life. In fact, all of this talk about finding financial freedom through investing in real estate in the last few chapters might even be leading you in that direction! While the goal of this book has been simply to make readers aware of the dynamics of personal changes, it is possible that the examples and illustrations that we have used may have peaked your curiosity. Whatever the case may be, it's important to remember that the Taking Action step of the Powerful Changes Process is all about making a complete commitment to positive change.

With that in mind, read the following examples of Taking Action and write down four action steps that you will take right away to begin to move yourself toward the better life you are dreaming of.

• A woman struggling with consumer debt decides that in order to move toward a debt-free life, she needs to cancel her credit cards and cut them up. So one morning, she sits down at her kitchen table with a pair of scissors, cuts her cards into pieces, and takes the first step toward realizing her dream of being debit-free.

• A man who is sick an tired of working for a company that doesn't appreciate his drive and abilities updates his résumé and mails it to three other companies that he would like to work for. By physically moving toward getting a different job, he has taken an action step that will help him get out of an unacceptable situation.

• A man who desperately wants to escape from the daily grind of the corporate world decides that pursuing a career as an active investor is the path that he wants to walk in his Powerful Changes Process. After having read a few books on the topic and attending a seminar that equips him to be an active real estate investor, he sets aside a Saturday, calls up a real estate agent, and begins to look for some investment properties to purchase.

Each of these action steps might seem like small steps in the grand scheme of things. However, it is important to realize that progress toward a better life is often made by taking several small steps, one after another, in the right direction. Take some time at this point to think about the actions that you need to take in order to pursue your vision of better life. Don't worry about the size or scope of the action. Whether it is a big action step or a small one, go ahead and Take Action at this point. You will be surprised at how excited even the smallest step can make you feel!

Chapter 7

Putting Your System In Place

The Refining Process

Gold rarely comes out of the ground ready to be minted into coins or fashioned into exquisite jewelry. It's not very often that silver is pulled out of a mine and then immediately put to use in fine table service or precious ornaments. Iron doesn't come out of the ground ready to be pounded into farm implements or shaped into carpenters tools. These metals, both precious and otherwise, have to go through a Refining Process before they are ready to be put to use.

The Refining Process burns out all of the impurities in a precious metal and reveals it in its purest form. Take gold for instance. Gold is heated until it liquefies. The impurities rise to the surface of the molten metal. This dross is then skimmed off the top or even burned off in some cases, and the result is a purified metal that is ready to be made into a wedding band, a watch casing, or a delicate chain. Without the Refining Process, the gold wouldn't be ready to be put to use in a piece of fine jewelry. The Refining Process is necessary.

The sixth step in the Powerful Changes Process is all about Refining. The Refining phase of the Powerful Changes Process is as important to discovering the path to a better life as the Refining process is to purifying precious metals. The best ideas, the most obvious doors, and even the most determined action steps quite often need slight adjustments as they are implemented as a part of a strategy to build a better life.

Refining often follows great discoveries and bold action steps. For example, Thomas Edison discovered that electricity could be used to bring light into darkness. As he tinkered in his workshop, Edison – one of the most prolific inventors of all time – Discovered a Door that would lead to a better life for people all over the planet. Edison determined that electricity could be harnessed and used to power a filament that could shed light on a room and replace the need for oil lamps entirely. Edison's groundbreaking discovery had the potential to change life on Planet Earth. However, while Edison's idea seemed good in theory, he had a difficult time when it came to turning his theory into reality. Edison tried several experiments to develop a filament and bulb housing that could actually maintain light for any period of time. Of course, we all know the end of the story. Edison finally invented a light bulb that was capable of handling the taxing demands of electricity. What many people don't know is that when it was all said and done, Thomas Edison had developed more than a hundred light bulbs before he found one that could deliver on his idea. The light bulb that he finally invented has transformed life on Planet Earth. As a matter of fact, chances are pretty good that you are reading this book by the glow of a light bulb that exists today because of Thomas Edison's hard work as an inventor.

Edison's tedious struggle to invent a light bulb perfectly illustrates the importance of the Refining phase in the Powerful Changes Process. As Edison made one adjustment after another in his quest to invent the light bulb, his willingness to refine his invention finally led him to the goal he was after. As people pursue their visions of a better life, quite often the path they choose to arrive at their goals have to be refined along the way. The willingness to adjust a strategy for building a better life is an essential element in bringing about the positive changes that a person truly wants to experience.

That's simply what the Refining phase of the Powerful Changes Process is. It's the point in the Powerful Changes Process at which people begin to adjust and fine-tune their strategies to build better lives. Once steps are taken along a path that leads to personal growth and self-improvement, new discoveries are made along the way. These new discoveries make it necessary to tweak action steps to account for the new information that is gathered along the way. In other words, as people step through the doors they have discovered and begin implementing their plans to build better lives, those plans often need to be tailored to meet the unique challenges of their unique situations. As people take action steps toward life change, obstacles crop up that require slight alterations in their courses of action.

During the Refining phase of the Powerful Changes Process people recognize the flaws in their plans and remove them, action steps are fine-tuned, and people experience the freedom of adjusting their strategies to meet their life goals. It's important to understand that there are very few "cookie cutter" approaches that will lead everyone who follows them toward a better life. Because everyone leads a unique life, even the best plans that have worked for hundreds of people often have to be slightly altered to meet the needs that individuals face. The truly great thing about the Refining step in the Powerful Changes Process is that it allows people to come to a better understanding of themselves as they customize their goals and plans for their own benefit. In other words, as people take steps in the right direction they also embark upon an amazing journey of self-discovery that allows them to get in touch with their personal likes and dislikes in a way that they never could before. Let's look at a couple of stories that show how the Refining step in the Powerful Changes Process works to bring about a better life.

John Burley's Refining Story

As Bryan interviewed one successful investor after another, he quickly noticed that all of them had gone through a period of Refining on their path to positive life change. All of them had made slight adjustments in their strategies to take into account their own individual needs, wants, and desires. Nobody's Refining experience illustrates the importance of this phase in the Powerful Changes Process better than John Burley's.

When John walked away from the financial planning industry to begin his career as a real estate investor in Phoenix, he was confident that his plan to create passive income by investing in real estate would work. At the same time, he would quickly discover that the niche that he had chosen to put his investing strategy into practice in needed to be Refined to meet his personal goal of having more freedom to use his time the way he wanted to.

In the world of real estate investing there are three basic strategies or niches that investors use to generate healthy returns from their investments. Some specialize in the "Quick Cash" strategy of real estate investing. In this strategy, an investor buys a home at a wholesale price, and resells it quickly at a retail price. The investor might make some low cost upgrades to raise the value of the property. He might paint the house inside and out, install new carpet, and spruce up the landscape. He might even add on a room. It all depends upon the desires of his market, the cost of repairs, the price at which he purchased the home and the price at which he will be able to resell it.

As an illustration, let's say an investor named Jim buys a home at a wholesale price for $70,000.00. Other homes in the area that happen to be in better condition are selling for $100,000.00. Jim buys the house at a wholesale rate and goes in and makes a few repairs. He paints, has the carpets cleaned, and brings in a landscaping company to fix up the yard. When it's all said and done, Jim has invested about $6,000.00 in upgrades and repairs to a house that he bought for $70,000.00. Jim has now invested $76,000.00 in this property. He puts it up for sale at $95,000.00. An eager buyer offers Jim $92,000.00 for the home. Jim accepts the offer and resells the home six weeks after purchasing it. He gets $92,000.00 and subtracts his costs of $76,000.00 and realizes that he has just made $16,000.00 in six weeks. That's the "Quick Cash" strategy of real estate investing, and a lot of people make a lot of money every year implementing that strategy.

John Burley did Quick Cash real estate transactions early in his career as an active investor. He liked the immediate cash returns he got from Quick Cash, but this strategy had one major flaw in it as far as John could tell. Making lots of money quickly was nice, but John was looking for a steady flow of passive income. With the Quick Cash strategy he had to go out time and time again, find homes for wholesale, do a few upgrades, and then remarket them for Quick Cash. As soon as the property was resold, it was no longer a source of income. In order to keep making money with this strategy as an investor, John realized that he would have to spend the rest of his life doing Quick Cash deal after Quick Cash deal. This strategy felt too much like a job to John. So he Refined his investing strategy.

John was confident that investing in real estate was the door that he needed to walk through in order to improve his financial situation for the long term. As he ventured into the world of being an active real estate investor, he simply needed to Refine his technique. So John decided to implement the second basic strategy for investing in real estate. He decided to adopt a "Buy and Hold" strategy as his preferred niche. The Buy and Hold strategy is simple enough to understand. Let's use our fictional investor, Jim, once more to illustrate this niche. Jim goes out and buys a $100,000.00 house a bit under market for $90,000.00. He does some minor renovations and turns around and markets it as a rental property. Jim's payment on this house is around $600.00 per month. He sets a rental price on it for $800.00 per month. Someone rents it at $800.00 per month. This difference in income is called the spread and Jim pockets it as long as he has occupants.

Jim continues to rent this house for five years. There are minor adjustments in the rental rate, and the house appreciates about 18% over those years. Now the house is worth $118,000.00. Jim's renters move out, and instead of renting it again, Jim sells it out right. Over the past five years, Jim has paid down the underlying loan of the house. He no longer owes the entire underlying mortgage. When Jim sells the house he pays off the underlying loan and pockets the appreciation on the house. So, Jim has got a decent spread from the house for five years and moderate appreciation. He walks away with some good money in his pocket. This is essentially how the "Buy and Hold" strategy works.

John Burley used this strategy as a real estate investor for a while. He made some good money at it. The only problem was that John quickly found out that being a landlord wasn't what he wanted out of life. Late night phone calls to unclog toilets, repairs to the properties because of reckless renters, and all of the other nuisances that go along with land lording were not John's idea of living a better life. John still believed that investing in real estate could produce the steady stream of passive income that he was looking for. He simply realized that once again he needed to Refine his investing technique.

So John looked around for another technique that would allow him to enjoy a passive income and at the same time free him up from being a landlord. That's when John decided to put the "Cash Flow" strategy to work for himself. The "Cash Flow" or wrap technique, as some call it, is remarkably easy to understand. Let's use our fictional investor, Jim, again to illustrate this technique.

Jim acquires a $100,000.00 house for a bit below market value for $90,000.00. He then finds an occupant who will become a tenant/buyer. Jim carries the financing for the new occupant since the new occupant can't qualify for a conventional bank loan. Jim's underlying payment on the house is $600.00 per month. He sells the home to the tenant/buyer for $925.00 per month. Jim pockets the spread of $325.00 per month and the buyer is now a homeowner. Since the occupants of the property are working toward owning and not just renting the house, they take much better care of it and are responsible for any repairs that the property might need. Jim is spared from all of the late night repair calls. He just has to collect his money, pay the underlying mortgage and deposit the spread in his bank account. Of course, there are adjustments to this concept that need to be made from state to state and country to country, but this is basically how the "Cash Flow" strategy of real estate investing works.

John Burley finally settled on the "Cash Flow" strategy to acquire a steady flow of passive income from his real estate investments. Since then he has gone onto to pioneer innovative strategies in his field of expertise. However, from the moment that John Discovered the Door of investing in real estate to generate a passive income, he never wavered from that path. He simply made adjustments here and there. John's basic strategy of achieving financial freedom through investing in real estate never changed. He simply Refined that strategy to meet his personal wants and desires so that it would truly work for him.

That's what the Refining phase of the Powerful Changes Process is really all about. It's making minor adjustments to a basic plan of action that will lead to a better life.

Craig Chandler's Refining Story

Craig Chandler went through a process of Refining in his Powerful Changes Process as well. Craig is an entrepreneur who lives in one of the most beautiful places in the world – the Gold Coast of Australia. Craig has been a business owner since his late teens. Early in his life he bought a piece of land and began growing trees and other decorative plants. Before too long Craig had a thriving nursery business that allowed him to make a decent living. But Craig new that he eventually wanted more out of life than just a decent living. He wanted to be able to step away from the day-to-day operations of his business so that he could spend his time doing the things that he wanted to do.

As Craig's business began to thrive he had enough sense to realize that simply spending the profits on stuff would not help him in the long run. So Craig began to look for solid investments that would generate great returns. Craig wanted to turn the profits from his business into growing investments that would speed up his retirement. Since Craig is a savvy businessman he didn't have to look far to realize that investing in real estate would provide him with a solid investment that would deliver a fantastic rate of return. Once Craig Discovered the Door of investing in real estate as a strategy to improve his financial situation and provide for his financial security, he was able to Take Action steps to build a solid investment portfolio. Craig began to look for properties to invest in. He found some good real estate investment opportunities and used them to generate a steady stream of passive income. Once he began to invest in real estate, Craig saw the potential it provided for financial freedom and security. At the same time, because he was still involved in his nursery business, Craig knew that he needed to Refine his real estate investment strategy to make it a better fit for the lifestyle he wanted to live. He didn't want to spend his time aggressively looking for solid investment properties. He just wanted a steady stream of passive income from a high producing investment portfolio.

Craig began to assemble a team. He talked to a local realtor, and explained the kind of properties he was looking for. He spoke to a loan officer at a bank and established a relationship with him that would make it easier to purchase investment properties. Craig then put this realtor and loan officer to work looking for properties that would suit his needs. Today, instead of looking for the properties and running the numbers on the loans, Craig gets regular calls from several people who are doing this work for him. All he has to do is accept or reject the properties and potential investments and then collect the passive income from his portfolio. By doing this, Craig has created a very successful investment system that provides him with a steady and permanent stream of passive income from his lucrative investments.

Craig's basic strategy of putting the profits of his company to work as capital for real estate investing never changed. When he Discovered the Door of investing in real estate, he knew that was the path he needed to walk in order to meet his financial goals. However, Craig did Refine his strategy along the way to better suit his lifestyle.

The Refining phase in the Powerful Changes Process allows people the opportunity to fine-tune their strategy for growth and development. While the stories in this chapter have shown how John Burley and Craig Chandler, one of John's Advanced Investing Boot Camp staff members, adjusted their real estate investing strategies for a better fit with the lifestyles they were after, the truth is that any major or minor life change involves a period of Refinement. When people move from a state of Dissatisfaction to a state of inner contentment, both major and minor adjustments need to happen along the way. The Powerful Changes Process opens people up to self-discovery. As people get in touch with what they really want out of life, they grow and evolve. What they were looking for at the beginning of the Powerful Changes Process has a tendency to change slightly along the way. That's why Refining is such an important element in the growth process. It allows people the freedom to adjust their life paths as they grow and develop as human beings.

Confident and Empowered

Like every step in the Powerful Changes Process, the Refining phase is characterized by it's own unique emotion. As people continue to take steps toward their fulfillment of their dreams, they still experience the excitement that accompanies the Taking Action phase of the change process. At the same time that excitement starts to evolve into empowerment during the Refining phase of the Powerful Changes Process.

Empowerment is an inner sense of self-confidence that comes as the result of positive experiences. When steps are taken in the right direction and a certain amount of success is achieved, people going through the Powerful Changes Process will begin to feel empowered. This inner sense of empowerment is only enhanced when people start to make the minor adjustments that go along with the Refining step in the process. Having enough knowledge and experience to know what adjustments need to be made shows real growth and development. As people Refine their strategies to better meet their wants, needs, and desires, they experience a sense of empowerment. They realize that they know enough about themselves and the strategies for change that they have chosen to make a few minor adjustments and Refine their courses of action. All in all, these realizations can fill people with a sense of confident empowerment. For this reason, the emotion that truly charac-terizes the Refining phase of the Powerful Changes Process is an inner sense of empowerment.

Action Steps

Before you move on to the next chapter, take a moment to go through these action steps.

The Refining phase is an interesting point in the Powerful Changes Process. It's during this phase of the change process when a person begins to experience a surge of self-confidence. A course of action that will lead to a better life has been chosen. Steps are being taken in the right direction. The Refining phase is the point at which a person truly believes that he has made the right choice. The unhappiness of the Dissatisfaction phase of the change process is a memory. And while a person hasn't "arrived" at what he eventually wants in life, at this point in the Powerful Changes Process he is confident that he will.

Now that you have read this chapter on the Refining phase of the Powerful Changes Process, take a moment to imagine yourself in the position to make minor adjustments to your change strategy. In the Action Steps at the end of Chapter 4, you were encouraged to paint a word picture of the kind of life that you truly want to live. With that word picture in mind, move through these simple action steps to catch a glimpse of the Refining step of the Powerful Changes Process in action.

1. If you are still in the Search phase of your Powerful Changes Process, take a moment to imagine that you have moved through that step of the change process, and Discovered the Door that will lead you to your better life.

2. Now imagine that you are taking action steps in the right direction. Your plan is working. You're experiencing the financial success or relational fulfillment that you want out of life. You're enjoying the spiritual depth that you truly want as a key element in your life.

3. Now that you know that Refining is an important part of the Powerful Changes Process, make a commitment that as you walk the path of your change process, you will take time every once and a while to re-evaluate your change strategy.

Maybe you have already moved through the Search phase of the Powerful Changes Process and Discovered the Door that you were looking for that will lead you to a better life. Perhaps you are even boldly Taking Action to achieve your goals. You've found the path that you are looking for and you are walking it. If so, take a moment to go through these actions steps.

1. Think about how you have grown and developed as a person since you began to make Powerful Changes in your life. List the four most significant changes that you have experienced throughout your Powerful Changes Process.

2. How close to your ideal life are you? Does the life you are living today look like the life you dreamed of when you began to ponder living a better life? If so, good for you. If not, take

a moment to think about a few minor adjustments that you could make that might move you closer to the life you are looking for.

3. Now write down a few personal actions steps that you could take to move closer to your vision of an ideal life.

The Refining phase of the Powerful Changes Process is an empowering part of personal development. In this phase of the change process, people gain that sense of empowerment and confidence that they need to sustain them as they work the plan that will move them toward the better life they are after. This sense of empowerment is what helps a person persevere as they continue to press on toward the fulfillment of their dreams.

Chapter 8

Perseverance – Letting "Lag" Assure Your Success

Incredible Perseverance

In a fantastic book entitled <u>Finishing Strong</u>, Steve Farrar tells a remarkable story of perseverance from the frontier days of the American West. It's worth sharing at this point in our journey through the Powerful Changes Process. It seems that one of the men who accompanied Lewis and Clark on their historic expedition across the America frontier in the early 1800's was a man named John Colter. When Lewis and Clark turned back to return home after completing their exploration, John Colter decided to stay on in the American West. He wanted to do some more exploring on his own. He wanted to paddle his canoe up some streams and get a really good look at this newly discovered land.

Colter survived in the American frontier by trapping animals and trading their pelts to the native people. He was the first white man to see the Geysers in what is now called Yellowstone National Park. John Colter saw some amazing sights, accomplished some amazing things, and along the way became a hero of the early American west.

Throughout his journeys, Colter was never very far from danger. He was attacked by grizzly bears, hunted by hostile Indians, and even threatened by the whitewater rapids that he encountered as he traveled up virgin streams and rivers. Through the years as people began to move west, John Colter became something of a living legend. His reputation preceded him wherever he went. He became a true folk hero to the Americans who were expanding their horizons and heading west to see what this new land had to offer.

However, one particular feat sealed John Colter's fate as a living legend. John Colter became extremely well known around dinner tables and campfires across America because of a foot race that he ran on one fateful day. Colter had been trapping along a river near what is now Bozeman, Montana. He was traveling with a friend of his named John Potts. When Colter and Potts paddled their canoe around a bend in the river, they heard some movement along the banks. Before they realized what was happening, they were surrounded by Blackfeet Indians. There was no time to escape downstream. Colter steered his canoe to the bank of the river and tried to get out and run. However, the Indians were faster than Colter and Potts. They were upon the trappers before they knew what happened. Potts jumped back into the canoe and tried to paddle away, but the Blackfeet filled him with arrows and ended his life.

John Colter was in deep trouble and he knew it. The Blackfeet warriors quickly captured him, stripped him, and debated about what to do with Colter. They entertained the thought of torturing him to death. However, the leader of the raiding party had other ideas. He approached Colter and asked him if he could run like a deer. Colter indicated that he was a slow runner. He lied. Colter knew that he could run like the wind. Still, the leader took Colter's bait and led the raiding party with their prisoner to a sandy patch of ground nearby. The leader made a mark in the sand and lined his warriors up. He then took Colter three hundreds yards ahead of the warriors and told him to start running. By this time Colter wasn't wearing any clothes or shoes. Those things had been taken from him when he was taken prisoner. So when the leader of the raiding party released Colter, he took off running bare-naked across the sandy plain.

Colter ran like lightning. He knew his very survival depended upon it. The plain extended out for about six miles from where Colter started. He ran as fast as he could. All the time he heard the warriors yelling behind him and trying to close the gap that separated them from the white trapper. It was understood that the warrior who caught Colter would have the sadistic pleasure of ending his life. As Colter ran he saw a line of trees on the horizon. He taxed his body to reach the trees before he was overtaken.

After running at a sprinter's pace for three miles, Colter noticed that only a handful of the warriors were still in the race. However, one warrior had gained on Colter and was now only about two hundreds yards behind him. By this time, Colter's bare feet were mangled from running over rocks and cacti. Nevertheless he kept running as fast as he could, ignoring the pain and pushing his body beyond its limits. When the warrior finally got within 50 yards of the trapper, John Colter spun around and faced his pursuer. The warrior was so surprised by Colter's brash move that he stumbled and fell as he threw his spear at Colter. The spear missed its mark, so Colter grabbed it, and quickly ended his pursuer's life.

Colter still had about two miles to go before he reached the line of trees he had been running toward. He knew that the Blackfeet Indians would not be content to let him get away. He knew they would hop on their horses and hunt the white trapper down. So Colter kept running. His body was screaming in pain from the extreme exertion, his lungs were ready to burst, his feet were mangled, and his heart was pounding. But John Colter persevered.

He finally reached the line of trees. He kept running until he came to a deep stream. Colter jumped into the stream and swam underneath a pile of driftwood that had gathered against a sandbar in the stream. The Blackfeet Indians quickly reached the icy stream. Fortunately, Colter had concealed himself so well in the icy waters of this flowing stream that he could not be found. Eventually the raiding party gave up its search.

After several hours of being submerged in the icy waters, Colter drug himself up onto the sandbar and collapsed. He was completely exhausted, suffering from hypothermia, and without food or clothing. Colter had no rifle and no horse, the elements of a basic survival kit in the frontier American west. However, Colter did have his life. So the next morning, when the sun came up and warmed his body enough so that he could move, Colter stood up and started walking. Seven days later he walked into the Bighorn trading compound naked and bleeding. By the way, the Bighorn compound was 150 miles from the stream that John Colter hid in to avoid being captured by the Blackfeet Indians[1]. Talk about incredible perseverance!

Tested By Time

What an amazing story of perseverance. It's that kind of persistence that inspires us to put up with the small nuisances of life. Most people will never have to run barefoot through the wilderness to save their lives. It's those kinds of stresses and hardships that make the minor irritants of life pail in comparison. At the same time, most people understand that achieving anything in life does require overcoming obstacles and putting up with nuisances until goals are reached. The simple fact of the matter is that pressing on toward a better life does require perseverance. For that reason, Perseverance is a necessary step in the Powerful Changes Process. In fact, Perseverance is the seventh step or phase in the process of moving toward a better life.

As a phase in the Powerful Changes Process, Perseverance is all about letting the actions that you have taken actually work for you. The Perseverance step of the Powerful Changes Process is the step during which life decisions and action steps are tested by time. The truth is that lasting Powerful Changes take time to happen. As a person moves toward his or her vision of a better life new habits need to be formed and healthy patterns need to be established. In an instant gratification society, many people expect a few initial steps to bring about tremendous results. While this does happen at times, lasting Powerful Changes often come as the result of the consistent and systematic application of action steps that will lead to the fulfillment of dreams.

There's really no flashy way to put this. The plain and simple truth of the matter is that lasting life change takes Perseverance, and Perseverance involves a certain amount of lag. What is lag? Lag is a principle best illustrated by the biblical concept of "reaping what you sow". In the New Testament letter of Galatians, the Apostle Paul wrote, "Whatever a man sows, this he will also reap... Let us not lose heart in doing good, for in due time we will reap if we do not grow weary". (Galatians 6:7b and 9). The idea behind

---

1 Steve Farrar, Finishing Strong (Sisters, Oregon: Multnomah Publishers, Inc., 1995). Farrar offers a fuller account of this event as well as a list of his historical sources on pages 189 through 193 and 222.

this ancient concept is very simple to understand. As people Persevere down a particular path, they will reap the benefits or consequences of following their chosen paths.

So if some choose not to make positive changes and choose not to grow and develop as people, they will simply become stagnant. On the other hand, people who have spent the time Searching for a path that will lead to positive life change and then take steps down that path will eventually get where they want to go. In the end, if people Persevere and don't turn aside from their chosen courses of action, they will move closer and closer toward the ideal lives that they are after. That's what lag is. Lag is simply following through on a plan long enough to reap its natural consequences.

P.T. Barnum, the great American entertainment entrepreneur, summed up the essence of Perseverance with this simple quip: "A constant hammering on one nail will generally drive it home at last, so that it can be clinched." Moving toward personal growth and self-improvement takes a willingness to keep hammering the nail of an action plan until it results in the desired effect. The simple truth is that life will provide you with plenty of challenges and obstacles to overcome. The biggest difference between successful people who continue to grow and develop as human beings and the average person who gets stuck in stagnation is really quite easy to identify. The people who are experiencing Powerful Changes view obstacles and upsets as a chance to grow and learn rather than as failures. And so they endure through them. They Persevere. They continue to work their plans because they know they have persevered in searching for the best way to bring about the fulfillment of their dreams. When handed a setback, rather than giving into fear and abandoning a good plan, people bent on making positive and lasting changes in their lives simply bolster their determination against the challenges and keep going. Eventually, the tried and tested systems and strategies that have been put into place gain momentum and do their jobs.

That's what the Perseverance phase of the Powerful Changes Process is all about it. It's about settling down and letting the action plan that you have developed as you have journeyed through the Powerful Changes Process do its work. When moving toward a lasting life change, you have to give a particular course of action enough time to work. Unfortunately, some people short circuit the Powerful Changes Process by not persevering. When obstacles and challenges crop up, as the inevitably do, instead of sticking to a good plan, many people abandon ship and look for a different course of action that will lead to a better life.

Sometimes it's important to re-evaluate a plan. If the steps you are taking toward a better life just aren't getting you to where you want to be, then there are times when it's important to look for a new plan. At the same time, too many people abandon good plans too quickly, because they don't experience instant results. Growth, change, and success all take time. That's why it is so important for anyone committed to making positive changes in their lives to be aware of the Perseverance phase of the Powerful Changes Process. Without giving your plan of action some time to work, you might miss out on a good thing.

Fortunately for Adrian, he hung in there and persevered when he began taking action steps to move toward a better life. Let's take a moment to look at Adrian's Perseverance story.

Adrian Oakman's Perseverance Story

It's been a couple of chapters since we spent some time looking at Adrian Oakman's story. You probably remember that Adrian was the dissatisfied dairy farmer who was working himself to exhaustion in a job that kept him too busy to be the father and husband that he wanted to be. Adrian came to terms with his Dissatisfaction and realized that he was standing at a crossroads in his life. His physical weariness and the burning desire deep inside of him to be more in control of his time and energy came to a climax when he experienced a Trigger Event that made him realize that something absolutely had to change in his life. Adrian then went on a Search to Discover a Door that would open onto a path to a better life. Adrian eventually found that door and discovered that if he spent his time, energy, and other resources on becoming an active real estate investor, he could step away from the dairy farm and devote his time to his family.

Adrian Took Action and attended John Burley's Advanced Investing Boot Camp, held twice a year in Phoenix, Arizona. He went home to New Zealand with all of the information and skills he needed to become a successful real estate investor. As soon as Adrian got home to his farm, he started to Take Action on what he had learned. Adrian began to look for investment homes to purchase. He started lining up some investment partners who believed in the strategy of remarketing houses to produce positive streams of passive income. Everything seemed to be falling into place. The action steps that Adrian set before himself were in fact leading him in the right direction.

At the same time, Adrian still had to perform his farming duties. Dairy cows still needed to be taken care of. Production on the farm had to go on as scheduled. Beyond that, Adrian had contracts that he needed to fulfill. So, as Adrian dealt with the burden of running a busy dairy farm, he refused to give up his plans of eventually leaving the farm and becoming an active and productive real estate investor. He knew that in order to take that step he would have to acquire a healthy portfolio of investment properties. So even though his body was taxed and desperately in need of rest, Adrian got up every day, performed his duties as a dairy farmer, and in the evenings pursued his career as a real estate investor. Adrian would work a twelve-hour day on the farm, seven days a week, and then turn his attention to his investment career after the evening chores were done.

Because of his Perseverance, Adrian's investing career started to thrive. He was purchasing homes on a regular basis. Buyers, who could not qualify for conventional bank loans, were lining up at his door to move into his homes. The system Adrian learned was working. He could see that investing in real estate would eventually allow him to step away from farming forever. However, the double burden of caring for a farm and becoming a successful investor was a massive drain on Adrian's time and energy. It would have been easy for him to give up along the way. After working all day long, Adrian simply wanted to spend some time with his family in the evenings. He could have easily made excuses to spend his evenings at home rather than spend them in his community acquiring and remarketing investment properties. But Adrian knew that if he gave into the temptation to give up on his plan of action for achieving a better life, he would regret it for as long as he lived. So Adrian Persevered. He hung in there through the tough times. He overcame the obstacles set before him. He pressed on to achieve his dreams. The day that Adrian stepped away from farming forever was a day of intense and emotion-filled celebration for his family. This celebration was only made possible by Adrian's willingness to Persevere. If he hadn't given his plan enough time to do what it was intended to do, he never would have experienced the joy of finding freedom. If Adrian had simply ignored the principle of lag and gave up when the hard work of moving forward set in, he would still be an exhausted dairy farmer barely making it in life rather than the prosperous and financially free investor that he is today. Fortunately for Adrian's wife and children, he is a man of incredible Perseverance.

Today Adrian is an incredibly successful investor who has acquired dozens of investment properties that generate a permanent stream of passive income for his family. He is living his dream life. His family enjoys the abundant time that he spends with them. Adrian has leisure time to pursue his hobbies. He even gives back by volunteering as one of the staff members at John Burley's Advanced Investing Boot Camp. If it weren't for Adrian's strong character and willingness to Persevere, none of these wonderful things would have become reality for him.

John Burley's Perseverance Story

There is also an up side to the Perseverance phase of the Powerful Changes Process. When a person finds a strategy to achieve success, sticking with that strategy results in sustained success. While Perseverance is an important element for overcoming obstacles, Perseverance is also a key ingredient in facilitating success. The truth is that people do "reap what they sow", and when a person is sowing for success the reaping can be sustained for an indefinite period of time if a person perseveres.

Unfortunately, it is not uncommon for people to sabotage their own personal improvement by bouncing from strategy to strategy too quickly. Sometimes people experience a little bit of progress toward a better life and then they stop taking steps in the right direction before they reach their full potential. When the success process is shortchanged before Perseverance has an opportunity to produce amazing results, the person journeying through the Powerful Changes Process can miss out on the full benefits. Rather than press on toward their personal dreams, some people become content way too soon and miss out on the fulfillment of their visions for better lives.

Few illustrate the power of Perseverance for sustained success better than John Burley. Once John Burley Discovered the Door of investing in real estate as a way to generate passive income, he acted on that strategy. When we looked at John's story in the last chapter, we discovered that he Refined his strategy over a short period of time. He moved from the "Quick Cash" strategy of investing into the arena of "Buy and Hold". After he realized that he didn't want to spend his time, energy, and money on being a landlord, John then Refined his strategy even further to focus almost exclusively on the "Cash Flow" strategy of real estate investing.

Once John discovered that the "Cash Flow" strategy of real estate investing was the niche that he would use to gain his financial freedom, he zeroed in on it as his primary investing strategy. He created and put in place systems that allowed him to acquire investment properties and remarket them quickly in order to produce passive income. John worked his system into a cookie cutter step-by-step process that consistently allowed him to produce positive financial gains time after time. Then he Persevered. He simply kept doing the same kind of real estate deal over and over and over again.

At this time an interesting thing began to happen. A variety of people who knew John kept telling him what he should do next, even though these people really didn't know what they were talking about. Some people told John that he should start buying apartments. Others told John that the really big money was to be found in commercial real estate. Others told John that if he wanted to make it big he should become a developer. It's interesting to note that John had a proven system that was making him money hand over fist, and yet all of these people who were essentially broke were telling him to change his system. They wanted him to stop doing something that was working very well so that he could start doing something that these advisors really knew nothing about. Fortunately, John understood that so-called advisors who offer opinions without actually doing what they are suggesting aren't authentic advisors at all.

John stuck to his proven system that was working well and reaped the benefit of a growing passive income. The steady stream of passive income kept getting bigger and bigger. Then one morning John woke up and realized that he was a millionaire. So he kept doing the same kind of deal time after time, until he woke up one morning and realized that he was a multi-millionaire with a passive income to provide a life of prosperity and abundance for himself and his family! After that realization, John continued to do the same kind of deal over and over again. He Persevered. Once he found financial freedom and experienced success as a professional investor, John continued to let the principle of lag increase and improve his financial situation. Today he continues to do hundreds of real estate transactions around the world each year using his proven system.

The simple fact is that Perseverance is a key ingredient in sustaining personal success and self-improvement. It's a critical step in the Powerful Changes Process. In the Perseverance phase of the Powerful Changes Process people can either set themselves up for greater success and continued growth or they can short circuit their paths to personal fulfillment.

Patient Perseverance

Like every phase of the Powerful Changes Process, the Perseverance phase is characterized by a particular emotion. If a person successfully avoids the temptation to sabotage the life change process and allows lag and Perseverance to produce positive changes, that person develops an inner sense of patience. Patience is an emotional willingness to wait. Patience is characterized by a calm sense of emotional steadiness that reveals an inner confidence that everything will ultimately be okay. Sometimes patience can be a difficult emotional discipline to develop.

Martin Luther, the father of the Protestant Reformation, was known to have prayed this prayer: "Lord, give me patience – NOW!" The truth is that patience can't be developed immediately, but it can be shaped out of the raw material of the confidence that comes from having faith that your action steps will lead you to the fulfillment of your dreams. In other words, if people are confident and they believe that they have Discovered a Door that will eventually lead them to the better life that they are after, then that confidence can result in emotional patience during the Perseverance phase of the Powerful Changes Process.

The enemy of patience is panic. In fact, panic is really the opposite of patience. It's panic that causes people to bounce from change strategy to change strategy as soon as an obstacle appears in their life path. As soon as people encounter setbacks as they implement their action steps, panic fills the mind with thoughts that maybe their plan wasn't such a good idea after all. On the other hand, patience can bolster personal confidence as one barrier is torn down after another.

There is a sense in which patience is really a choice. When it comes to the Powerful Changes Process, patience is the conscious decision to resist panic. Patience is the personal choice to manage anxiety and uncertainty in a healthy way. Should anxiety levels rise on the road to a better life, patience is the emotional stabilizer that encourages a person to hang in there while knowing that better things are just around the corner. For that reason, patience is the emotion that most commonly characterizes someone who is pressing on through the Perseverance phase of the Powerful Changes Process.

Action Steps

Before you move on to the next chapter, take a moment to go through these action steps.

The Perseverance phase of the Powerful Changes Process is so important when it comes to bringing about positive changes in our lives. Unfortunately, some people sabotage themselves as they try to fulfill their dreams. They let panic cause them to bounce from one life path to the next without ever letting the principle of lag do its work. The key to staying the course during the Perseverance phase is to maintain emotional patience by having faith in your plan to bring about positive changes in your life. Take a moment to move through the following action steps as you begin to develop the skills you will need to stay the course.

1. The best way to maintain patience while moving through the Perseverance phase of the change process is to focus on your vision of the way you want your life to be. We will spend some time talking about visioning in a later chapter. For now, take a look at the response you wrote to action step 2 in Chapter 2. In this action step you were encouraged to write brief descriptions of what you want your all off the major areas of your life to look like. Review what you wrote.

2. After having read this far in this book, take some time to flesh out those written descriptions a little more. Be as specific as you can possibly be.

3. Now place your written descriptions in an area where you can regularly review them. Make an appointment with yourself to read these written descriptions of how you truly want your life to be at least once a week. This will help to keep you focused on the goals you are moving toward. This focus will help you patiently Persevere as you continue to pursue your dreams.

Now that you have worked through the first seven steps of the Powerful Changes Process, chances are pretty good that you are beginning to understand that positive change is doable and continued personal growth is a lifelong process. Perseverance and persistence are important ingredients that have helped people make lasting changes for the better throughout human history. The people that we most admire and the stories that fill us with deep inspiration are often stories of remarkable Perseverance. John Colter, the legendary American frontiersman, Persevered under amazing hardship and eventually became revered as a hero of the American West.

Anyone who perseveres and persists on their path to build a better life is a true hero. In a world that too often settles for mediocrity, people who pursue lives filled with meaning and joy are the true heroes of our times. At the same time, people who press on through the Perseverance phase of the Powerful Changes Process have realized the fact that pursuing meaning and joy is really a lifelong process of Continued Growth. With that in mind, let's turn our attention toward talking about Continued Growth in the next chapter.

Chapter 9

Getting Better

A Missed Opportunity

The story of the American railroading industry is a story of missed opportunities and the failure to evolve. When trains first started pushing their way through the great American frontier they completely revolutionized travel for Americans. Journeys that used to take months on horseback could be completed in a matter of days by railroad. The railroads really changed life in America and opened up new possibilities and opportunities on the western frontier.

But the railroads didn't only change the way Americans traveled. They also changed industry in America. After the railroads were developed people could get the goods and services that they wanted. The railroads connected the coastlines of America and made it possible to ship supplies back and forth across the United States in a very efficient way. Building materials, cattle, cotton, and all of the other staples that formed the economic foundation of the modern American economy became important building blocks because the railroads could easily ship these things from coast to coast. On top of that, new towns and cities grew up along the railroads that eventually populated the interior of America. The railroads changed everything.

The railroad industry also made a lot of people a lot of money. Railroad moguls built enormous personal financial empires from the huge profits they were raking in year after year. For a time, railroad men were among the wealthiest men in America. They controlled transportation, shipping, and the distribution of resources across the country. However, today the railroad industry in America pales in comparison to its former glorious self. Many of the companies that became financial titans because of their roles in the railroad industry have fallen from prominence. Many of these corporations no longer exist at all. How could such massive financial machines fade away into nothingness in a matter of a few decades?

Economic experts believe that the railroad empires that created vast financial fortunes and incredibly lucrative businesses faded away because of missed opportunities. In other words, railroad companies went out of business because they didn't keep up with the times. They didn't continue to grow and develop as corporations. The major downfall of the railroad industry in America happened because railroad executives didn't realize what business they were in. They thought they were in the "railroading" business. In reality, they were in the "transportation" business.

Railroads served one simple purpose. They moved things and people from one place to another. And when new and better methods of transportation started to develop in America, the railroad companies kept doing what they had always done – railroading. Many of them didn't expand to incorporate new technology. As a result most of those companies do not exist today.

Making Change An Ally

When people and companies fail to grow and develop, they become stagnant and eventually obsolete. In the world of biology, living beings – plants, animals, and people – that stop growing simply die. Human beings continue to grow and develop new cells as long as they live. The same is true for plants and animals. The only kind of being that is not "growing" in some way is a dead being. Growth means life and abundance. When things stop thriving, it is usually because they are dying.

This principle applied to the concept of the Powerful Changes Process helps us understand that Continued Growth is a necessary part of a life that is thriving. For that reason Continued Growth is the eighth and final phase of the Powerful Changes Process. As people seeking better lives begin to realize the fulfillment of their dreams, Perseverance urges them to stick to their chosen paths. They know that if they stay the course they will continue to experience positive results. At the same time, people who are becoming more self-aware as the result of working through the change process usually begin to realize that they need to stay open in order to constantly evaluate their lives. Regular self-evaluation can keep a life from growing stagnant and becoming stuck in the quagmire of mediocrity. Regular self-evaluation can even open people up to new possibilities and an even better vision of what life could ultimately be. To put it simply, finding even a small amount of personal fulfillment can expand a person's horizons and fill that life with new hope for an even better future.

Once people gain some distance from the unhappiness experienced during the Dissatisfaction phase of the Powerful Changes Process and begin to experience the patience and peace that come from confident Perseverance, new horizons open up in life. People become free to explore new territory and as a result discover new possibilities for what life could be in its full potential. This constant self-evaluation and the openness to look for new areas of life to pioneer form the essence of the Continued Growth phase of the Powerful Changes Process.

The Continued Growth phase of the Powerful Changes Process represents the phase during which people achieve a better life and recognize that they always need to be open to the process that led them to where they now are. Once they make the changes that make their lives better, they become open to the power of change to transform and improve their lives. So, during the Continued Growth phase of the Powerful Changes Process one should stay wide open to the possibility that more changes may be necessary in the future. In actuality, during the Continued Growth phase of the change process, most people begin to expand their horizons by looking for new ways to grow and develop as human beings.

It's important to recognize the huge shift that this phase of the change process represents in the evolution of a human life. Think about this for a moment: when a person initially steps into the change process, it is usually in response to the pain of Dissatisfaction. Once that person has worked through the Powerful Changes Process and found relief from the Dissatisfaction and even fulfillment from achieving a goal or dream, that person starts to embrace and even invite change. An amazing transformation has occurred. Before, change was simply something that needed to happen for survival and sanity, but once the Continued Growth phase of the Powerful Changes Process is reached, change is embraced as a force that can bring about great joy and peace in life. Change itself becomes a tool for positive results rather than a necessary step for survival.

This evolution of a person's perception of change is an important byproduct of the change process. Many people are adverse to change. They get so comfortable with the paths that they are walking along that they wear ruts in those paths and eventually get stuck in those ruts. The result is that when change becomes absolutely necessary it is often so difficult and uncomfortable that they can't take the necessary steps to make their lives better. On the other hand, people who have worked through the Powerful Changes Process can arrive at a point where they are no longer adverse to change, but instead actually looking for opportunities to make positive changes. For the person who has moved through the Powerful Changes Process and grown as a result, change is no longer the enemy - it's an ally!

Joe Arlt's Continued Growth Story

You remember Joe Arlt. He's the guy who had the corporate job that most business school graduates would covet. Joe spent his young adult years traveling for a company that greatly benefited from his expertise. He made a good living as a budding young executive, and yet the world of business travel, the constant pressure to perform, and the shark-like attitude of many executives in the corporate world began to weigh heavily upon Joe. He had dreamed of becoming the chief financial officer for a Fortune 100 company. All of those dreams changed one day when he realized that he didn't want to be like the CFO's he had met. He didn't want their lives.

As Joe moved through the Powerful Changes Process after being spurred on by a Trigger Event experience and the Search for a path that would allow him to excel in the business world without forfeiting his personal life, his Dissatisfaction was eventually replaced by peace and fulfillment. Once Joe discovered the path to financial freedom that actively investing in real estate could provide for him, he set up systems and implemented his plan until he achieved his goal. Joe Refined his strategy over time, but ultimately he Persevered in his particular niche and became a sought after personal mentor and financial educator.

Somewhere along the way as he kept pressing on through the Perseverance phase of the Powerful Changes Process, pursuing his strategy as a real estate investor, Joe realized that he had the systems in place that would allow him to experience financial freedom for the rest of his life. At the same time, because he had moved through the Powerful Changes Process, he began to see that change is a powerful force that can be harnessed to bring about positive results in a person's life. Because of this shift in the way he perceived change, Joe was wide open to the possibilities that his new life afforded him.

When he began to consider how he could continue to grow and develop as a human being, he was gripped by a strong conviction to help the human community with the wealth that he had created. Not only that, because Joe has become such a successful investor, he realized that rather than simply give money to charities, he could develop some investments that would generate long-term passive income for the charities of his choice. When John Burley approached Joe Arlt about developing a tape set that could serve to educate people about the techniques that had led to Joe's success, Joe jumped at the opportunity. He soon decided that all of the profits gained from the sale of this tape set would go toward helping charities that are actively out there easing the suffering of people on Planet Earth.

Joe's desire to continue to grow as a person opened him up to the possibility of becoming a force for good in this world. Today, Joe is an incredibly successful real estate investor who has an investment portfolio of more than five hundred real estate properties. He continually acquires new properties in an effort to grow this portfolio. At the same time, Joe has come to believe that he needs to put his investing abilities to work in order to make this world a better place. Joe sees change as his ally and uses his abilities to benefits countless others. That is the essence of the Continued Growth phase of the Powerful Changes Process. Once a person begins to see change as an ally, new possibilities open up, horizons are expanded, and truly amazing things happen.

Steve Dover's Continued Growth Story

Like Joe Arlt, you have already met Steve Dover. He was the hardworking Australian businessman who spent his time and energy working hard for a company that was so caught up in profit margins that it dropped the ball when it came to appreciating its employees. You'll remember that Steve grew up dreaming of becoming a millionaire businessman. In the early stages of his pursuit of that dream, he followed the conventional path in his search for financial freedom. Steve was taught in school that if people want to get ahead in the world, all they have to do is get a decent white collar job working for a big company and climb the corporate ladder to financial bliss. Steve was beginning to suspect that millionaires weren't made that way. Then one day after his company merged with another his suspicions became convictions based on facts.

Steve's Trigger Event moment occurred when he walked into his company's new office building and discovered that the only difference between his work cubicle and the cubicle of the brand new employee was that Steve's cubicle had a cabinet and the other worker's did not. At that moment, Steve finally realized that the conventional path to financial freedom and prosperity was not going to work for him. He needed to find another way to fulfill his dream of becoming a millionaire businessman.

After a time of searching, Steve stumbled upon John Burley's financial wisdom. Steve attended a seminar that John held in Australia designed to teach people solid money habits and open them up to the idea of creating passive streams of income through investing in real estate. Steve's mental light went on and he decided that he would take the necessary steps to become an active real estate investor. Steve took action by attending John Burley's Automatic Wealth course and then the

Advanced Investing Boot Camp as a student. Steve then went home and immediately began to implement the investment skills and strategies that he learned at John's seminars.

Now, just a few short years later, Steve really is a millionaire businessman. He has acquired hundreds of investment properties and has become one of the most successful, innovative and productive investors in the cash flow real estate niche in Australia. He Refined the techniques that he learned from John Burley to meet his particular needs and desires. Not only has Steve established a lucrative real estate investing firm, he has also established his own mortgage company that allows him to meet his clients' needs by providing them with a house and the financing they need to acquire a home.

Steve has persevered. He has set systems into place that insure his continued success and allow the principle of lag to do its work. Today, Steve lives a wonderful life that includes surfing several days of the week and spending quality time with his family and friends. Through building and growing his businesses, he has a creative outlet that allows him to exercise his entrepreneurial spirit. On top of that, Steve has assembled an amazing team of people who understand his financial goals and personal values and work hard to keep his companies growing.

Once Steve realized his dream of becoming a millionaire businessman, he allowed the Perseverance process to continue to grow his businesses. At the same time, he began to view change as a friend and an ally. Once he looked up and scanned the horizon of possibilities after reaching his own personal goals, Steve realized that he was in a unique position to do a lot of good for a lot of people. Beyond traveling to Phoenix, Arizona twice a year to volunteer as a group leader at John Burley's Advanced Investing Boot Camp, Steve has added another dimension to the Continued Growth phase of the Powerful Changes Process that is truly inspiring.

Since Steve figured out the hard way that true financial freedom is seldom gained by the conventional route of working hard for a company and climbing the corporate ladder, he vowed not to treat his employees as he had been treated by the company he used to work for. So, when Steve started to build a company that focused on investing in real estate, he found a team of young men and women and made a deal with them. He told them that if they would work hard for him, he would work hard for them. He established it as a goal during the Continued Growth phase of his Powerful Changes Process that he would work hard to make sure that the people who work with him would have the opportunity to become millionaire businessmen and businesswomen.

Steve's strategy is simple. He trains his people to become real estate investors. They acquire and sell properties for him. At the same time, they have opportunities to acquire and sell properties for themselves. To put it simply, Steve insures that his people acquire investment properties for themselves so that they can build a steady stream of passive income that will allow them to become financially free and prosperous like Steve is.

Some people would see this as a bad business move. Some would want to keep all of the real estate deals they stumble upon for themselves. Not Steve. He believes in the principle of abundance. There are basically two approaches to understanding resources. Some people hold to a theory of scarcity that says that there are only so many resources to go around. People who hold to this view go around trying to acquire as many resources for themselves as possible while preventing others from getting any for themselves. After all, if others are out there struggling to acquire the same resources, they might take all of the resources for themselves. This is scarcity thinking, and most people and economists on Planet Earth hold to this theory because of a limited scope of reality.

The other approach to understanding resources is the abundance theory. People who hold to the abundance theory of resources believe that resources beget resources. In other words, as people procure resources they use them most of the time to create new resources. So, in fact, there really are more than enough resources for everyone to have plenty. If competition occurs, it will only serve to improve selection for people. In fact, economists agree that free market enterprise and healthy competition actually serve to build economies and create resources rather than place limits or ceilings on what can be accomplished. The abundance theory teaches that there is enough to make every person on this planet financially abundant and prosperous. Steve, and people like John Burley and the other Advanced Investing Boot Camp staff members that you have read about in this book hold to the abundance theory. It is this approach that allows Steve to work for the personal financial freedom and prosperity of the members of his team.

Steve's Continued Growth story is inspiring because it shows how one man moved through the change process and realized how powerful change is to bring about positive results in people's lives. But Steve didn't stop with this realization. This realization caused him to develop a plan to help his team members experience their own Powerful Changes through the path that he has chosen. Steve began to see change as his ally and he wanted to help the people closest to him make positive changes in their lives as well.

The Continued Growth phase of the Powerful Changes Process capitalizes on the good results that have happened so far in the change process and pushes people to move forward and experience more of what life truly has to offer. Few Continued Growth stories illustrate that dynamic better than Steve's.

The Satisfaction of Moving On

The Dissatisfaction phase of the Powerful Changes Process is characterized by a sense of unhappiness that can range from slight irritation to downright despair. The Trigger Event that pushes people to move out of their discomfort zones carries with it a sensation of anger that compels a person to change. When a person moves into the Search phase of the Powerful Changes Process they often experience feelings of fear. The fear of failure or even the fear of success can accompany a person's Search for a better life. However, once a person Discovers the Door that opens onto the path that leads to a better life that fear is often replaced by relief. When a person begins to Take Action toward fulfilling lifelong dreams, relief becomes pure excitement. When action steps are refined during the Refining phase of the Powerful Changes Process, feelings of excitement become feelings of empowerment. When people continue to work the plan they have developed that will lead them to further growth and personal success during the Perseverance phase of the Powerful Changes Process, all of the emotions surrounding change prepare that person to experience emotional patience.

Every phase of the Powerful Changes Process is accompanied by a characteristic emotion. The strength of these emotions will vary from person to person, but everyone will experience them to some degree. One way to determine where you are in your Powerful Changes Process is to reflect on the emotions you are experiencing. Are you feeling strong emotions of fear? Maybe you are still in the Search phase of the change process. Are you experience an overwhelming sense of empowerment as you fine-tune your strategy to build a better life? Then chances are pretty good that you are in the Refining phase of your change process.

How can a person know when he or she has arrived at the Continued Growth phase of the change process? When people reach the point where massive change has already taken place and they are basking in the victory of taking the rights steps while at the same time viewing change as an ally, they have reached the Continued Growth phase of the Powerful Changes Process. When the overwhelming emotion you experience as you ponder the area of your life that needed be transformed is a tremendous sense of satisfaction and contentment, chances are good that you have reached the Continued Growth phase.

The key emotion that defines the Continued Growth phase of the Powerful Changes Process is an inner sense of satisfaction. It's important to understand at this point that satisfaction doesn't necessarily mean stagnation. Life is growth. As stated earlier in this book, when a living being stops growing, it is in the process of dying. So once people arrive at the Continued Growth step in the Powerful Changes Process and begin to experience true satisfaction and contentment, that doesn't mean that they will never long for or aspire to greater things. That's just a part of human evolution and the spiritual make up of the people God has placed on this planet. At the same time, satisfaction over achieving a goal, fulfilling a dream, or accomplishing something spectacular is a common experience during the Continued Growth phase of the change process.

The great thing about experiencing satisfaction and contentment at this point in the change process is realizing that your emotions have come full circle. Where dissatisfaction and discontentment once existed, walking through the Powerful Changes Process can minimize those emotions and replace them with their exact opposites – satisfaction and contentment. So in a very real way, and certainly on an emotional level, the Continued Growth phase represents that last phase of the Powerful Changes Process.

With all of that in mind, it's important to understand that people should not come to a point in their lives where they simply decide to stop changing and growing. Again, life is about growth and change. People who resolve to stop growing and evolving as human beings are quickly on their way to becoming out of touch with life and stuck in ruts that can eventually lead to stagnation. To put it simply, people who are adverse to change are always going to be uncomfortable in a changing world. Everyone who lives on Planet Earth in the twenty-first century is swimming in the waters of change. It's all around us. One of the most important secrets to thriving in an environment of change is to adopt the position that change is a powerful ally that can produce amazing results. People who have reached the Continued Growth phase of the Powerful Changes Process know that truth very well. As a result, they experience a great deal of contentment and satisfaction in life.

Action Steps

Before you move on to the next chapter, take a moment to go through these action steps.

If you are currently in the Continued Growth phase of the Powerful Changes Process, take some time to go through these action steps so you can take advantage of the energy you have generated on your path to a much better life than you have ever lived.

1. On a scale of 1 to 10 (1 being the lowest degree and 10 being the highest), where would you rate the strength of your belief that change is your ally?

2. If you highly rated the strength of your belief in the fact that change can be an ally in your life, chances are that you are well prepared to reach the Continued Growth phase of the Powerful Changes Process. Assuming this is the case, take a moment to reflect on your life and consider how you could take advantage of the power of change to bring about a greater degree of success for yourself.

3. The most important skill to develop that will empower you to thrive in the Continued Growth phase of the Powerful Changes Process is the ability to view change as your ally. You have most likely made positive changes in the past that have led you into a better life. Take a few moments and list all of the ways that being willing to change has improved your life in the past. This little exercise should help you see that change really has been your ally as you have walked the path of your life.

4. Viewing change as your personal ally to build a positive future for yourself, begin to think of some things that you could do through the power of change to make a positive difference in the lives of people around you. In the stories related in this chapter, you came in contact with Joe's passion to make the world a better place and Steve's passion to help the people in his life experience the financial success that he already enjoys. What would you do to move beyond yourself in the Continued Growth phase of your change process to bring positive elements into the lives of others?

It is possible that you have already worked through the steps in the Powerful Changes Process on many occasions. Since change is such an integral part of a thriving life, the odds are that you have already experienced a series of positive changes throughout the course of your life that have made you the person you are today. At the same time, odds are very good that as you continue to grow and develop as a human being, you will experience the need to change in other areas of your life as well. Since that is the case, let's spend some time looking at the habits that promote positive change in a person's life.

Chapter 10

Four Keys To Powerful Changes

Developing Healthy Habits and Beliefs

One of the most important skills to acquire in life is the ability to develop healthy habits. Our habits are our routine behaviors. They are our usual manner of doing things. Habits are those ingrained patterns that define what we will do on any given day and how we will react to any given situation. Believe it or not, habits are surprisingly easy to develop. Experts in human behavior tell us that if a person does something on a regular basis for between twenty one and twenty eight days in a row, then that person has developed a habit. For instance, if a person gets up and does some kind of exercise every morning for three to four weeks, then exercise becomes a habit for that person. If a person reads for a half hour every day at the same time of day, then reading will become a habit.

On the flip side of the coin, if people resolve to break a bad habit and stick to that decision for three to four weeks, the odds are very good that they will be able to overcome even the most harmful of habits. One of the most common "bad habits" that plagues many people is nail biting. Many people confess that they have gotten into the bad habit of biting their fingernails for whatever reasons. Sometimes nail biting is a manifestation of inner anxiety. Sometimes nail biting is just evidence of boredom. Most of the time, nail biting is just habitual. But if people can abstain from biting their nails for three to four weeks, experts in human behavior say that the bad habit of nail biting can be broken. Good habits are easy to develop and many bad habits can be conquered in just three to four weeks' worth of time. And yet habits define our lives. They determine how we are going to react in many situations and how we are going to spend our time. Habits can be great supporters in our quests to build better lives for ourselves and for our families.

For that reason, it's important at this point to identify the healthy habits and patterns that can help people promote Powerful Changes in their lives. These habits will serve as the keys to promoting Powerful Changes in your life. Our study of successful people who have moved through the Powerful Changes Process has revealed to us four basic habits that have enabled people to maintain personal success and fulfillment. Some of these habits are simple behaviors. Some of the patterns are habitual ways of thinking that have instilled a sense of direction and confidence in the people who practice them. Since we are primarily concerned with the ability of our readers to master the change process and use Powerful Changes to their advantage, we are going to take some time at this point to reveal the habitual behaviors and beliefs that can promote Powerful Changes. While you are reading these next few pages, begin to think of ways that you can implement these patterns of behavior and belief into your own life to insure your personal growth and development. At the end of this chapter, we will provide some specific action steps you can take to begin developing the healthy habits that have enabled successful people to stay at the top of their games.

Habit #1 – Surrounding Yourself With Supportive People

The first habit that is essential to promoting Powerful Changes in your life is the practice of regularly surrounding yourself with a supportive group of people. Our peers have a great deal of influence over us because our peers make up our group affiliations. Human beings are social beings who form groups for the sake of comfort, support, and security. Over time those groups develop their own set of values and mores. When a member of a group begins to step outside of the boundaries of the group's values, often the group will exert pressure to make that straying member conform to social norms. Our groups can be our families, our churches, our civic clubs, our golfing partners, or even our neighborhood associations. We crave these informal group associations because they give us a sense of identity and companionship as we move through life. People put a lot of stock in their peer groups. Why? That's just how people work, because we are social beings who like to belong to groups.

Since our group affiliations have such a profound impact on our personal values and priorities, it is so important that we associate with supportive and optimistic people as we move along the path toward a better life. Unfortunately, this world is filled with pessimistic people who quite often try to keep others from breaking out of the chains of pessimism and finding success and joy in life. One of the tragic mistakes that many people make on their road to a better life is listening to all of their potential critics along the way. Many people get sidetracked before they ever start moving down the path to a better life because they make the mistake of putting too much stock in the silly advice of unsuccessful people. As people start to make Powerful Changes in their lives, those who are unwilling or unable to break out of the unhealthy habits that keep them from living life to the fullest will do their best to keep people stuck in the mire with them.

Often when a person feels compelled to make a major change in life, he unavoidably finds himself surrounded by people who don't understand the inner transformation process that he is going through. As a result, these people often fail to support the positive changes that this person is trying to make in his life. Why are some people so critical and unsupportive? This is an incredibly complex question, but it is worth exploring for a moment.

Like Father, Not Necessarily Like Son

Some people are naturally critical of people who are trying to make Powerful Changes in their lives, because they don't want to admit to themselves that they are unhappy in their own circumstances. For instance, let's say a father who happens to be a factory worker has ingrained in his son that he should grow up to be a factory worker. Let's say this father isn't really all that satisfied with the life of factory worker, but he settles for it anyway because his job at least provides him with a steady income and a week or two of vacation every year.

If this father were completely honest with himself, he would admit that he would love to toss off the shackles of shift work in a factory and pursue his dreams of an easier, more balanced life. However, over the years the father has numbed himself to the dissatisfaction he experienced as a younger man just so he could tolerate the boredom and drudgery of the way his life eventually turned out. This father encourages his son to walk the same path that he has walked in life not because he believes it's the best way to experience a life of fulfillment but because subconsciously the father believes that if his son follows the path that he himself chose this will somehow validate the compromises that he has made along the way. Sounds complex, doesn't it? It really isn't. The simple fact of the matter is that some people don't want others to succeed because this sometimes points the spotlight on their own personal failures – or so they think.

Let's say that in our hypothetical story, the son simply refuses to walk the path that his father trod before him. This son knows that deep down inside his father isn't really all that happy. Besides, the son doesn't want to spend his days doing repetitive work, worrying about the occasional labor strike and tolerating the days between his brief vacations. So this son moves in a completely different direction. Maybe he decides to go to college to train to become a literature professor. The father resists this idea. Maybe the father even goes to the extreme of ridiculing his son's dreams and aspirations. Deep down, the father envies the son for his passion and the courage that it takes to pursue something meaningful. At the same time, the father subconsciously knows that to acknowledge that he settled for less is simply too painful to come to terms with. As a result, the father remains unsupportive and critical of his son's professional aspirations because supporting them would mean that the father might have to recognize that he wasn't brave enough to step out and take a chance on pursuing his own dreams in life.

This scenario gets repeated all over Planet Earth every day because some people honestly believe that the successes of others will somehow cast a disparaging light on their own personal failures.

The Green-Eyed Monster And It's Even More Evil Twin

Another reason that explains why some people are so unsupportive when others attempt to break the shackles of mediocrity is the age-old issue of jealousy. Jealousy has been called "the green-eyed monster" by some because of the sheer ugliness that it brings to human relationships. Jealousy is simply wishing that you had what someone else has. Of course, this kind of jealousy can cause things like possessiveness and even a lack of trust in human relationships. However, when it comes to the personal achievements of others, jealousy can quickly turn into its even-more-evil twin, envy. Envy is an advanced degree of jealousy. The best way to understand envy is to see it as jealousy pushed to its most unhealthy extreme.

When a person is jealous, he wishes that he had what his friend already has. When a person is envious, he also wishes that he had what his friend already has, but this inner wish gets pushed to an extreme and takes an ugly twist. Since he doesn't have what his friend already has, he wishes that his friend didn't have it either. Did you catch the subtle twist that resulted in the distinction between jealousy and envy? Jealousy causes a person to wish for something that he doesn't have. Envy causes that same person to wish that others didn't have what he doesn't have.

There is a subtle distinction between jealousy and envy, and both emotions cause many people to be unsupportive of others who are trying to get more out of life. Jealousy and envy are ugly twins. Envy is a bit more evil, because it is certainly more destructive in terms of its effects on human relationships.

Your Own Unrealistic Expectations

There are certainly other reasons that motivate some people to be unsupportive of those who want to excel in life. One of those is your own unrealistic expectations. In other words, sometimes unrealistic expectations cause us to see a lack of passion in others as a lack of support. It's important to understand that as you move through your Powerful Changes Process you will certainly encounter people who aren't as excited about your personal growth as you are. In some ways it is unrealistic to expect people to feel the same intense passions about your personal growth and progress as you do. Only you understand the intensity of your

Dissatisfaction. Only you know how relieved you were when you finally Discovered the Door that opened onto a path that would eventually lead you to the better life you are living.

Powerful Changes are most meaningful to the people experiencing them. It's unrealistic to expect anyone else, even the people closest to you, to feel as strongly about your Powerful Changes Process as you do. Without understanding this, you will be tempted to see a lack of passion for your personal growth in others as a lack of support for you. For some, this can start to feel like a personal attack, and before too long relationships could be irreparably damaged. Avoid this trap. Understand that no one will be as excited about your personal progress as you will.

Find Safe People

Those are a few of the reasons why some people are unsupportive when others around them start to experience a certain amount of personal growth and success in life. The antidote to being surrounded by unsupportive people as you move through the Powerful Changes Process is to intentionally seek out a handful of supportive people. Supportive people, or safe people, can give you the encouragement and inspiration you need to move forward and find meaning and fulfillment in life. It is so important to surround yourself with safe and supportive people, because one of the ways we process information while we are moving through the change process is by talking about what we are experiencing. Without safe people who are supportive of you, you won't have anyone to bounce your ideas off of.

Habitually surrounding themselves with supportive people has been a key ingredient in the continued success of John Burley's Advanced Investing Boot Camp staff members. In fact, one of the things that John's staff members look forward to the most during Boot Camp is being able to spend a few minutes here and there with other people who are following the same life path that they have chosen. As they interact, share ideas, and encourage one another, the staff members experience a level of support that they don't get anywhere else. This mutual encouragement often influences the staff members to excel even further in their lives. In a very real way, the Boot Camp staff members have developed their own community that provides them with the support and encouragement they need to press on in their Continued Growth and development.

When John Burley noticed the power of mutual encouragement and the importance of being surrounded by supportive people, he established a Discussion Forum on his website, www.johnburley.com. Thousands of people have found encouragement, support and a real sense of community by plugging into John's very active Discussion Forum. An entire community of "safe people" is as close as the internet for the people who are pursuing their financial freedom through implementing John's money steps as taught in his international best-selling book, _Money Secrets of the Rich_, and his real estate investment strategies as taught at the Advanced Investing Boot Camp and in so many of his educational products.

Surrounding yourself with safe and supportive people is so important when it comes to making significant changes in your life. Peer pressure is a powerful force in our lives. It can encourage us to step out in faith toward a better future or it can shame us into settling for status quo. The influence of supportive people who spur us on to believe in ourselves and take positive action steps can make all the difference as we transform our lives for the better.

Habit #2 – Visioning

A vision is a clear mental picture of a better future. Beyond that, a personal vision of the way you want your life to be can be a powerful motivator as you move through the Powerful Changes Process. Most people have some idea of what they would like their lives to look like if all things were equal. At the same time, most people convince themselves that, for whatever reason, their lives will never be they way they wish they were. In other words, most people have a dream about their ideal life, but few people pursue those dreams because they convince themselves that dreams never come true. This is an incredibly sad state of affairs, because most people could fulfill their dreams and make their lives better than they are, if they would only take some time to define a plan of action and follow that plan.

One of the most important motivators for people who are pursuing their dreams is a very clear mental picture of what their lives will one day look like when their dreams come true. As people visualize the lifestyle that they plan to live once they reach their goals, they get a little taste of what their lives will one day be like. Quite often, that little taste is enough to keep them moving toward "the whole enchilada". A vision of a better life is a necessary element in the Powerful Changes Process. This vision becomes the finish line toward which people are racing as they make progress in the change process.

It's important to understand that a vision is different than a goal. A goal is an achievable and measurable task that can be performed. A vision is more than that. It is a mental portrait of how life will be. Let's illustrate this concept with an issue that touches most people. Many people carry entirely too much consumer debt. Credit card balances, car payments, and department store charge cards take much of what the average worker makes on a weekly basis. For that reason, a lot of people have identified as one of their chief financial goals the desire to get out of debt. So, they set a goal of getting out of debt. Since goals needs deadlines in order for people to pursue them, most consumers who set the goal of getting out of debt usually attach a date to that accomplishment. So the goal ends up looking something like this for the average consumer bent on becoming debt-free: I will pay off all of my consumer debts within eighteen months from now.

That's a goal. A vision is different because it imagines what life will be like once that goal is met. Let's say someone is spending around $900.00 per month in debt reduction so they can achieve the goal of becoming debt-free. As they move toward that goal they are really pursuing a vision of what life will be like once that debt is paid off. The person pursuing that goal is thinking about what he will do with an extra $900.00 per month to spend. He is imagining how it will feel to have the burden of debt lifted off of his shoulders once and for all. He is also probably thinking about how he will invest some of that money to build a better future on a long-term basis. Maybe that better future will include retiring while he is still young and traveling to some exotic spots that he has always wanted to see. In reality, he is painting a mental picture of what his life will be like once he has reached his goal. That mental picture is called a vision.

Do you see the difference between a goal and a vision? A goal is measurable step. A vision is a mental picture of an achievable future of what life will be like once the goal is reached. And once again, a vision is an important motivator that helps people press on through the Powerful Changes Process in order to fulfill their dreams. A vision of a better future has always been an important motivator for people. In fact, the great Hebrew ruler, King Solomon, understood that once people lose their vision of a better future, they lose their hope and even their desire to persevere through the tough times of life. In the Old Testament passage of Proverbs 29:18 in the King James Version of the Bible, wise and wealthy King Solomon wrote, "Where there is no vision, the people perish." People need to have a keen awareness of what life will be like when they are spiritually, financially, relationally, physically, and professionally everything that they could be. This vision keeps us from losing hope and losing the desire to grow and evolve as people.

Throughout this book you have been encouraged to imagine what your life will be like as you move through the Powerful Changes Process. We've been talking about a "better" life and even an "ideal" life. Action steps have encouraged you to imagine what your daily schedule will look like when you achieve the goals that you have set for yourself. If you've taken time to do the action steps, you have even gone into detail with your mental portrait. You have an idea of what your life will actually look like in the future. As you have imagined this life, you might have even felt some of the feelings that will one day make up your emotional environment. Maybe you have felt the relief of being out of debt or the freedom of being in control of your time and energy. These mental images and emotional feelings form the vision of your better life.

One of the most powerful habits that you could ever develop as you continue to grow is the habit of visioning on a regular basis. Many of the successful people that make up John Burley's Advanced Investing Boot Camp staff told Bryan that they regularly take some time out of their lives to sit and imagine what their lives will be like when they fulfill their dreams. Some of these people have pictures of the places that they want to visit one day taped to their bathroom mirrors. These pictures serve as visual reminders every day. Some have pictures of their dream homes or their ideal cars that they look at several times each day. These simple pictures serve as reminders for these people to focus on their visions of better lives as they face each day.

Highly successful people and people who have realized their dreams and goals in life are usually singularly motivated by a vision of the way they want their lives to be. Take some time to develop the habit of visioning as you make every effort to make Powerful Changes in your life. This habit will keep you focused on why you are striving for change in the first place.

Habit #3 – Rehearsing Your True Priorities

A habit that is closely related to visioning is the habit of rehearsing your true priorities. Our priorities are essentially the things that we value in life. Some people put family at the top of their priority lists. Others put a devotion to God at the top of their lists of priorities. Others place financial security or relationships with friends at a high level on their priority lists. Every person on Planet Earth – and we do mean "every" – has a set of priorities that defines what they do with their time each and every day.

Even people who spend their days in a subsistence level existence have priorities. People who live in struggling Third World countries might define their priorities in terms of basic survival. The daily allotment of time in these countries usually revolves around taking care of basic human needs. But this doesn't mean that people who live in these situations don't have a set of priorities that defines what they do from day to day.

Different people have different sets of priorities. In fact, our priorities are as unique as we ourselves are. What is important to one person might not be important to somebody else. However, what is important to everybody is taking time to define personal priorities. If people never make lists of the things that are important to them, then chances are good that they will end up neglecting the things they truly value while spending time focused on life's little urgencies. Defining your priorities is important at the outset of the Powerful Changes Process, because as you enter the Search phase of the change process, your priorities will in large part define the type of life path you are looking for as a solution to your Dissatisfaction.

Our priorities are closely related to our visions of the lives we want to live. For instance, if a person sets his family – his wife and children – at the top of his priority list, then chances are good that his vision of a better life will include spending quality time with his family. Since visioning is such a powerful motivator for people who are looking to make significant changes in their lives, it stands to reason that rehearsing priorities also plays a powerful role when it comes to staying motivated. Once our priorities are defined, taking some time each week to reflect on the things that are truly important to us can keep us focused and moving in the right direction.

Some people rehearse their priorities by looking at a priority list on a regular basis. That list might include things like family, friends, professional success, financial freedom, spiritual vitality, and a host of other key elements that make life worth living. Whatever the contents of the list may be, many people choose to keep a priority list close at hand so they can look at it regularly.

For many people, the most important things in life aren't really things at all. For many people, people are their priorities. They understand that when life is boiled down to its essence, it is all about a series of either healthy or unhealthy relationships. One person interviewed for this book chooses to fill the credenza of his desk with pictures of the people who are most important to him. Every day when he steps into his office to pursue professional excellence and make decisions that will shape his future, he stares into the faces of the people who will be directly effected by his decisions. By doing this, he is regularly rehearsing his priorities. This little exercise, which has really just become a part of his lifestyle, keeps him focused on the most important elements of his life.

One of the most important habits that you could develop to promote Powerful Changes in your life is to pick up the habit of regularly rehearsing your priorities. If you haven't taken the time to define your priorities, then you know where to start. Sit down with a piece of paper and pen in hand and make a list of the things that are the most important elements of your life. Then put that list in a place where you will see it on a regular basis. After that, make sure you pay attention to that list by regularly rehearsing your priorities.

Habit #4 – Remembering To Believe

James Freeman Clarke observed, "All the strength and force of man comes from his faith in things unseen. He who believes is strong; he who doubts is weak. Strong convictions precede great actions." Clarke was right. One of the most important habits to develop in the quest to bring positive changes to your life is the ability to habitually believe in yourself, your system, your vision, and your dreams.

Belief is a key ingredient in reaching the goals that you set for your life. One key obstacle that keeps people from achieving great things in life is a lack of belief. People strive to accomplish amazing things, because in some way they believe they can. If they didn't believe, they wouldn't try. Belief precedes action. This principle holds true when it comes to the Powerful Changes Process. People take steps to make positive changes, because they believe that their actions will produce great results. People who are making Powerful Changes are people who believe that they can reach their goals and experience the freedom that comes from controlling their own destinies.

When it comes to developing a life change strategy, growing and evolving people learn to believe in themselves, their ideas and their systems. For example, Bill Gates believed in an idea, and his ability to revolutionize the world with that idea. He followed a course of action that he believed would lead him to where he wanted to go, and this belief resulted in Gates achieving incredible wealth! Warren Buffet believed in his ability to turn $500.00 into a personal fortune in excess of $30 billion (not to mention the enormous wealth he has generated for his investors)! Belief precedes action. As you take steps to implement a strategy that will help you build a better life, make sure that you remember to believe that what you are doing is good. Believe that the skills you have developed to implement your Powerful Changes strategy have equipped you to become the person you want to be while you are living the life you want to live. Believe in your ideas. Believe in your vision. Believe that you can build a better life as you move through the Powerful Changes Process.

As we saw at the beginning of this chapter, our habits are our routine behaviors. They are our normal ways of doing things. Habits are those ingrained patterns that define what we will do on any given day and how we will react to any given situation. We can develop healthy habits that will actually promote Powerful Changes in our lives. Surrounding yourself with supportive people, visioning, rehearsing your true priorities, and remembering to believe are all beneficial habits that will go a long way to helping you realize your vision of a better life. Resolve now that you will make the effort to ingrain these behaviors until they become instinctual habits. You will find that these habits will serve you well as you travel down the path to build the life you have always dreamed of living.

Chapter 11

Breaking Through Barriers

Overcoming Obstacles

As we saw in the last chapter, there are a handful of action steps you can take to develop the habits that will help promote positive change and growth in your life. Unfortunately, the flip side of that coin is also true. There are also behaviors and beliefs that can prevent positive growth and change. One of the best ways to overcome these obstacles is simply to be aware of them.

When professional golfers prepare for a big tournament, one of the first things they do in order to get ready is play a practice round on the course where the tournament will be held. They do this because they want to get familiar with the layout of the course, the speed of the greens, and the feel of the fairways and rough. Professional golfers also play practice rounds because they want to become familiar with the unique obstacles of the courses they will be playing on. Every golf course is a like a fingerprint. Each course has its own set of bunkers, water hazards, and peculiar slopes that are designed to challenge golfers to play their best in order to win tournaments.

These obstacles serve an important role in a golf tournament. They weed out the mediocre players and give the great players a chance to flex their professional muscles. In other words, a mediocre player looks at a sand trap and sees an obstacle. A great golfer looks at a sand trap and sees a chance to take a risk, hit an amazing shot, and pull ahead of the pack. A mediocre golfer looks at a water hazard as an obstacle. A great golfer looks at a lake on a golf course and sees a challenge that if negotiated correctly could bring great rewards.

Life is filled with surprises that can be viewed as debilitating obstacles or challenges for potential greatness. And since life in the twenty first century is really a series of one change after another, it stands to reason that the change process is filled with its fair share of challenges and obstacles. The key to turning these challenges into opportunities is simply being aware of them in the first place. That's what makes the difference for professional golfers. As they play a practice round they become aware of the potential obstacles ahead of them on tournament day and plot a strategy that will allow them to excel. They turn these obstacles into opportunities. So, in reality, awareness can mean the difference between a good round of golf and a great round of golf for a professional golfer.

Awareness can also mean the difference between success and sustained status quo when it comes to facing potential obstacles on the path to a changed life. For that reason, let's take the opportunity to reflect on some of the obstacles that commonly prevent people from making Powerful Changes in their lives. Coming to terms with these potential obstacles here and now will serve you well as you begin to move down the path to positive change. Look at this chapter as a practice round before you step into the tournament of positive and lasting change. Let's consider the potential obstacles that prevent positive growth and change one by one so you will have a good idea of what you might face as you move toward a better life.

Obstacle #1 – A Lack Of Understanding

The bulk of this book has been designed to serve as a map for people who are interested in bringing positive growth and change into their lives. We've spelled out in detail the geography of the Powerful Changes Process. We've identified the path that most people walk as they move toward a better life in a simple step-by-step manner. You've been given a detailed look at each step or phase of the Powerful Changes Process. We've talked to you in theory, but we have also shared concrete examples of people who have taken the steps to build better lives. We've done this so that you will have a good understanding of the practical and emotional landscape that you will face as you take the necessary steps to build a better life for yourself and your family. So, in a very really way, we've drawn a simple map that will coach and guide you through your life change process.

The funny thing about maps is that they are only helpful if you know where you are to begin with. If you don't have an awareness or understanding of where you are currently located in relationship to the map you hold in your hand, then that map is useless to you. A map is really just a collection of lines and symbols that won't do you any good if you don't know what those lines and symbols mean. Many people step into the change process without an understanding of the geography of the change process or an understanding of where they are in the change process itself.

This lack of understanding is an obstacle that gets in the way of people who truly want to build better lives for themselves. After reading this far in this book, you have a grasp of the different phases of the Powerful Changes Process. People who don't have the understanding that you now possess often flounder in life. They spin their wheels and dwell in unhappiness without ever taking the necessary steps to move from Dissatisfaction to personal fulfillment. For that reason, a lack of understanding when it comes to the dynamics of the Powerful Changes Process can keep people from making progress in their quest for more out of life. To put it another way, people who don't have a basic knowledge of the map of the geography of change won't progress as quickly through the change process. In fact, they might get sidetracked completely at pivotal points along the path.

You now have that basic map. You even hold in your hands a guide to the emotional signposts that will keep you moving in the right direction. You now know that every phase of the Powerful Changes Process is characterized by its own distinct emotion and feeling. Being aware of those emotions and feelings will, of course, help you understand where you are in the change process and even give you some clues about what to expect as you continue to take steps in the right direction. Here's a quick reminder of those distinct emotions. You might want to get very familiar with these emotional signposts so you can keep track of your personal progress.

- Step 1 – Dissatisfaction – Unhappiness
- Step 2 – Trigger Event – Anger
- Step 3 – The Search – Fear
- Step 4 – Discovering the Door – Relief
- Step 5 – Taking Action - Excitement
- Step 6 – Refining - Empowerment
- Step 7 – Perseverance – Patience
- Step 8 – Continued Growth – Satisfaction

Moving through the change process with a clear awareness of where you have been and what you can expect to encounter along the way will help you overcome the obstacle that a lack of understanding can place in your path. You might even find it helpful to keep a list of these signposts handy so you can look at them regularly along your path to growth. These signposts will help you successfully navigate the geography of change.

Obstacle #2 – A Lack of Knowledge

The second obstacle along the path to Powerful Changes is a lack of knowledge. This obstacle is closely related to a lack of understanding when it comes to the Powerful Changes Process. However, it is slightly different. When people encounter the obstacle of lacking an understanding of the Powerful Changes Process, they are struggling to understand what is happening to them. When people encounter the obstacle of a lack of knowledge, they are confronting the fact that they aren't equipped to take action toward positive change.

For example, let's say a man decides that he wants to find financial freedom. Let's say this guy even has the sense to realize that one of the keys to discovering financial freedom is becoming debt-free. Unfortunately, this person yearning for freedom from the trap of consumer credit has absolutely no idea how to implement a debt reduction strategy. So he resolves to get out of debt, makes a feeble attempt at paying off a charge card, but when he sees very little progress after a few months, he gives up in despair. Some people might be tempted to label this man's problem as a lack of personal discipline or a self-control deficiency. However, in reality he simply lacks the knowledge he needs to develop and implement a debt reduction plan.

A lack of knowledge keeps a lot of people from implementing sound strategies that would carry them toward better lives. What's the solution for overcoming the obstacle of a lack of knowledge? You don't have to be a rocket scientist to realize that the solution for overcoming this obstacle is becoming a lifelong learner. The fact of the matter is that we all need to be lifelong learners if we are going to face the challenges of a rapidly changing world.

Sociologists estimate that the body of knowledge – the sum total of all of the information that is known on this planet – doubles every five to six years. In other words, six years from now there will be twice as much stuff to know as there is today! By the way, this is why encyclopedia sales are at an all time low. Back when encyclopedias first began to be published, they were marketed as near complete collections of all of the knowable information in the world. Today, the global body of knowledge is so vast that to produce an accurate encyclopedia that contained all of the known information in the world would be nearly impossible. Beyond that, if such an encyclopedia were published it would already be out of date by the time it hit the shelves. What's the moral of this little story? Simple. None of us will ever get to the point where we can stop being committed to lifelong learning. We all need to stay open to receiving new information and allowing it to expand our horizons.

All of John Burley's Advanced Investing Boot Camp staff members achieved their financial freedom and a greater degree of personal fulfillment by receiving more knowledge. Some learned a new skill that allowed them to approach their business ventures in a new way. Some picked up some new information that shaped the way they viewed consumer credit. Some got educated about different investment strategies available. As a result they revised their personal principles of investing. Receiving education was a pivotal part of their progress toward a better life. The remedy for

---

For a FREE 20 Page Report on

"How To Become Debt-Free In 3 To 7 Years On Your Current Income"

Visit www.johnburley.com.

---

the obstacle of a lack of knowledge is obvious. Being open to learn new things is an invaluable skill that will help you overcome this all too common obstacle.

Of course there are some simple ways to develop the outlook of a lifelong learner. Lifelong learners are readers. They frequently pick up books on a variety of topics that keep their mental thought processors fresh and their minds receptive to new information. Lifelong learners do things like attend seminars, listen to tape sets, and watch intellectually stimulating television shows to keep themselves informed of what is going on in the world and what new information they can pick up and assimilate into their lives. Being a lifelong learner will allow you to overcome the obstacle of a lack of knowledge as you walk the path toward a better life.

Obstacle #3 – A Lack of a Healthy Self Image

There are people who never step out onto the path to a better life because they don't believe that they are capable of greatness. For a variety of reasons, many people don't think very highly of themselves. Maybe they were fed a line by different people in their lives that led them to believe negative things about themselves. Maybe as children their teachers, peers, and unfortunately maybe even their parents interjected lies into their lives that have caused them to believe that they are worthless and of very little value in the grand scheme of things. Maybe a little league baseball coach called a little boy a failure when he struck out at bat, causing that little boy to grow up into a man who in the back of his mind believes that he is a failure. Maybe a little girl brought home a less than perfect report card from school one day and her mother called her dumb without thinking of the damage such comments make, causing this little one to grow up into a woman who believes that she is not smart enough to make the necessary changes that will ultimately make her life better. The fact is that many people walk around with an unhealthy self-image and a very low sense of self-esteem for a variety of reasons.

Of course, it stands to reason then that one of the most common obstacles that prevents people from moving out of their discomfort zones and stepping onto a path that leads to the fulfillment of their dreams is an unhealthy self-image. Some people believe the interjections planted in them early in life so strongly that they are paralyzed when it comes to pursing excellence in their adult lives.

However, it's important to understand that negative thoughts about ourselves don't just come into our lives when we are children. Plenty of negative beliefs about our personal value, abilities, and worth creep into our heads as adults. These interjections happen in a variety of ways. When a corporation downsizes, the people who lose their jobs hear the very clear message that they are not necessary and important. When a college student receives a failing grade in a class, he walks away believing that he might just be an all around failure in life. People received negative messages about themselves on a regular basis. Depending upon their personal inner health, these messages can cause deep wounds to form in their spirits that unfortunately leave them open to further wounding in the future. All of these messages can cripple a life by filling a person with an unhealthy and negative self-image.

When it comes to the Powerful Changes Process, this unhealthy self-image can keep people from stepping out of their discomfort zones and looking for ways to build better lives. If people believe that they are losers or failures, they will avoid taking risks because they don't want to open themselves up to the pain of further failure and potentially validate what they already believe about themselves. So an unhealthy self-image can really keep people from stepping out, taking risks, and making the changes that they need to make in order to fulfill their dreams.

How do you overcome an unhealthy self-image? That's a complex question. The answer to that question really depends upon how unhealthy the self-image is. Sometimes people need some quality help from a qualified therapist to overcome the obstacle of an unhealthy self-image. By the way, there is absolutely no shame in recognizing that need in your own life and even seeking the help of a great counselor. Counselors are experts in understanding how the human mind works. They go to great lengths to educate themselves. They apprentice under other psychologists who train them in the art of listening for the messages behind our words. Counselors have done a lot of people a lot of good. So, if you are thinking that you might need to talk to a counselor as one of the steps that you need to take in order to overcome your lack of a healthy self-image, don't feel any shame about that. The truth of the matter is that some of the bravest people on the planet are people who recognize their need for help and then take courageous steps to receive that help.

At the same time, it's important to understand that an unhealthy self-image can be greatly improved by the power of positive affirmations. Affirmations are simply truth statements that we speak into our lives that positively counteract the negative interjections that we have received over the course of our lives. For instance, if you have been led to believe that you are a perpetual failure in life, a positive affirmation that you might say to yourself on occasion could be something like this: "I have the power to succeed in life." These simple little truths statements can be such powerful tools when it comes to combating the negative messages that our minds send to our spirits at times.

Affirmations are powerful. They are also ancient in origin. In fact, one of the most revered and respected sacred texts of all time, the Bible, is filled with positive affirmations designed to bolster its readers during the tough times of their lives. In fact, in Psalm 8:5, the ancient Hebrew author tells his readers that God crowned men and women with majesty when He created them. In other words, people are the pinnacle of creation, and the most precious beings on Planet Earth. What an affirmation!

Many people find it helpful to place written affirmations in places where they can regularly see these positive messages so that they receive constructive encouragement on a regular basis. At the risk of sounding too much like pop psychologists, we want to encourage people to tap into the power of affirmations as they move along their life paths. Since the lack of a healthy self-image is something that keeps so many people from making Powerful Changes in their lives, we want to encourage you to go to whatever lengths are necessary to overcome the negative interjections that have plagued your past so you can press on toward a brighter future. Take advantage of the power of affirmations as you move through the Powerful Changes Process. If you would like to read more about the power of affirmations we suggest that you read Chapter 22 of John Burley's _Money Secrets of the Rich_. This chapter is filled with positive affirmations that have helped many people move toward the better lives they want.

We can view obstacles as either paralyzing problems or potential opportunities for greatness. As we move forward in our quests for better lives it is important for us to be aware of the most common obstacles that keep people from fulfilling their dreams. A lack of understanding, when it comes to the dynamics of the Powerful Changes Process, can trip people up. A lack of knowledge in terms of the skills and information necessary to make progress in any area of your life can also inhibit a person's potential. A lack of a healthy self-image can keep a person from ever taking the risks that are necessarily involved in making Powerful Changes. Be aware of these obstacles and don't let them hold you back as you move toward everything that life has to offer you.

Conclusion

Putting The Power of Change to Work

Throughout this book you have met a variety of people who all have one basic element in common. Their common element isn't an issue of backgrounds. You've noticed that the people you have read about in the pages of this book come from a variety of backgrounds. The common element that unites them isn't even an issue of personal values or priorities. The desires and dreams of the people whose stories you have read are all unique and different. The common element that connects these lives isn't even an issue of a common investment strategy, though many of them have chosen a similar path to secure their personal financial freedom. The common element that binds these stories together is simply the Powerful Changes Process.

All of the people that you have read about in the pages of this book walked the same path as they sought to make their lives better. All of the people who have been featured in these pages stepped out of their varying degrees of discomfort and onto the path toward a changed life. Today, each of the people featured in this book enjoys a life that is better than it was before they embarked on their journey through the Powerful Changes Process.

Do all of these people live their ideal lives? A few do. Most of them are still in process and still reaching out to grasp their personal visions of a better life for themselves and their families. Those who have fulfilled their initial dreams of a better life have discovered new dreams along the way that urge them to continue to grow and develop as human beings. Along the way, most of them figured out that life is a journey that carries us through one change after another as we grow and evolve into people equipped to fulfill their destinies.

Of course, that revelation should come as no surprise to you at this point. As you have read through the pages of this book, chances are good that you have figured out that continued growth and change is the true essence of life. Because this is true, we've gone to great lengths to map out the simple steps that are involved in the Powerful Changes that you will experience.

Most moves to grow and develop begin with a sense of discomfort, dissatisfaction, and discontentment. As people look at their lives and become aware of greater possibilities, a certain sense of Dissatisfaction begins to grow and develop in the human heart. Sometimes alleviating this discomfort is as simple as fine-tuning a daily schedule or improving the health of a significant relationship. Sometimes alleviating this Dissatisfaction means stepping out into a new adventure in life or pursuing a new career path. But once the Dissatisfaction is felt, a Trigger Event (which could vary from mild to drastic in nature) usually follows which begins a Search for something better.

This Search will ultimately result in the Discovery of a Door that opens onto a path that leads to something better. Walking down this path toward a solution for alleviating the discomfort requires a person to Take Action. These initial action steps require some courage as people step out in faith believing that a better life awaits them at the end of the Powerful Changes Process. Strategies are usually Refined along the way as the seeker discovers new things about himself and the plan that he has devised. But ultimately Perseverance does its work, the principle of lag sets in, and a person discovers a sense of satisfaction as he steps into the Continued Growth phase of the Powerful Changes Process. People who have gone through this process begin to see change as an ally for building a better life. With this mindset, they are able to harness the power of change and put it to work for themselves.

Of course, you already know all of this. You have read through the chapters of this book and grasped the basic principles and concepts of the Powerful Changes Process. You have come to an understanding of how it works. You have even taken some action steps that have put you out in front of the pack when it comes to making the changes that will lead you to a better life. You have even become aware of the habits that can be of tremendous benefit to you as you move through your Powerful Changes Process. You now understand how important it is to surround yourself with supportive people who can encourage and affirm you as you pursue the fulfillment of your dreams. You know that visioning – developing a clear mental picture of what you want your life to look like someday – can be a powerful source of inner encouragement and motivation as you move forward in your journey through the change process. You know that having a clear sense of your true priorities in life and rehearsing those priorities on a regular basis will keep you focused on the prize of a fulfilling life. You even understand how important it is to develop a belief in yourself, your skills, and your dreams as you take bold steps toward your personal progress.

You've even learned to be a realist as you recognize that your path toward your better life will be littered with occasional obstacles. At the same time, you have already taken steps to remove some of those obstacles. You know that a lack of understanding when it comes to the dynamics of the change process can slow people down as they take steps to make Powerful Changes. But you have developed a solid understanding of the change process, so this obstacle has really turned into more of an opportunity for you than anything else. You know that a lack of knowledge can cripple some people as they look for opportunities and strategies to build better lives. So you have committed to being a lifelong learner. You are going to stay on top of your game by accessing the information you need to make real progress in life. You also understand that the lack of a healthy self-image trips some people up before they ever take steps toward their dreams. Negative interjections throughout their lives keep many people from believing in the amazing potential of themselves. Knowing this has made you aware that positive affirmations can encourage and support you along your path to change. In short, you understand the obstacles and you have the tools to overcome them.

So what's left? A lifetime of self-discovery and personal success as you move toward the fulfillment of your dreams. You have the knowledge. You have the mental and emotional tools that you need to take steps in the right direction. The only thing left is to step out on the path to a better life by entering into the Powerful Changes Process. You can harness the power of change and put it to work for yourself to build the life that you have always dreamed of living. The truth is that you are an amazing person with boundless capacities and enormous potential to pursue and achieve your goals and dreams. We have written this book to help you do just that. We have spelled out what years of research have shown us about the process that carries people toward lives of meaning and fulfillment. We want you to benefit from our research. We want you to achieve your dreams. And we know that you can. So harness the power of change. Put it to work for yourself today, and live the life that you have always wanted to live. Here's to your personal Powerful Changes. Thank you and God bless!

About the Authors

John R. Burley

John R. Burley has achieved what most people would consider impossible. Starting out with little money, a workable plan of action, and a lot of desire, John was in a position to retire by the age of 32. Today, his investment portfolio includes an ownership interest in over 1,000 properties, stocks, businesses, and more. He invests in over a dozen US states along with two other countries through his internationally renown investment company "The Shield" which is dedicated to defending, protecting and providing the regular person of Planet Earth with the opportunity to "own their own home.". Internationally, John is known as one of the greatest "Cash Flow" Investors alive.

Referred to as "One of the Premier Investors in America," on US National Television, John has also been named in Who's Who of American Business People and International Entrepreneurs. Prior to becoming a full-time investor, John ran his own successful financial planning company and has vast knowledge in the areas of finance, investments, corporate tax reduction techniques, asset protection and real estate.

As the #1 Best Selling author of _Money Secrets of the Rich_, and many other information products and seminars, in today's information age John's material has literally been shared with millions of people throughout the world. He truly believes that everyone can achieve a rich, full life, filled with prosperity and abundance. He writes and teaches in a very straight-forward, easy to follow step-by-step way that makes learning how to become rich fun and easy. In addition to managing his investments and running his businesses, John regularly tours and teaches throughout the world in places such as North America, Australia, New Zealand, Southeast Asia conducting seminars on achieving financial freedom and happiness.

When not on vacation John, along with his wife Shari and their two children John, Jr. and Danielle live in the Phoenix, Arizona area. He is a passionate and committed family man, a top golfer and avid sports fisherman.

John R. Burley is a rare breed indeed. A man that practices what he preaches, John only started teaching his systems and techniques after he had become successful. The information he shares in his books and teachings come directly from real-life experiences that have worked time and time again for himself and countless thousands of students from around the world. He only teaches that which factually has been proven to work by him and can readily be adopted by others. He continues to earn and maintain the respect of the investment community because he is out in the "Real World" doing investment transactions on a day-to-day basis. In other words, John R. Burley is a man who "Walks his Talk."

Bryan K. Fergus

Bryan K. Fergus has spent his entire adult life helping people experience personal fulfillment as a Spiritual Director. He has served in professional ministry as a pastor for more than twelve years, and has also been a seminary professor, published author, and sought after conference speaker. Bryan holds a Master of Divinity degree in Biblical Communication, a degree that requires its holders to develop proficiency in theology, communication skills, ancient languages, and character development. Due to his years of experience and extensive education, Bryan has become an expert in the interpretation of ancient sacred texts. He can fluently read ancient languages and understands the intersection of ancient wisdom with a life of meaning and fulfillment in the modern world. Not only that, Bryan knows how to communicate spiritual truth in an easy-to-understand way.

Bryan is currently directing his energy toward serving the human community through speaking ancient wisdom into the marketplace of contemporary ideas. Bryan is the creator and author of the groundbreaking tape series *The Spirituality of Wealth.* He is a recognized expert in the field of understanding the important connection between a person's inner spiritual life and daily financial practices. Bryan is the Executive Director of Icon Resources International. This role enables Bryan to travel and speak internationally on the topics of personal spiritual renewal, harnessing the power of change, and understanding the intersection of spirituality with a healthy financial outlook. In this role, Bryan is helping people develop spiritually sensitive approaches to becoming financially prosperous.

In addition to his active professional life, Bryan is an avid reader, devoted kayaker, and empathetic listener. Bryan and his wife Debi live in Phoenix, Arizona with their three children - Tristen, Tess, and Timothy.

John's Acknowledgments

Powerful Changes! is the result of more than 25 years of my real life experiences in business, investing, studying and teaching. I would like to acknowledge the many people who offered their love, guidance, loyalty, integrity and support over the years.

Before, I thank these great people I would like to thank God for providing me with the blessed life that I lead and the ability to complete books such as this. I know that without His blessing and guidance this work never would have been attempted.

Now to the people, first of all thank you to my best friends, my family. Thank you to Shari, my wife of 10 plus years, whom I love so passionately and deeply. Thank you for your love, strength and support. For believing in me and standing by my side all those years ago when I dragged you away from your home and family to Arizona to become a real estate investor with me. To my next two best buddies, my son John, Jr. who has grown into such a fine young man and always puts a smile on my face and in my heart, and my daughter Dani, who brings me so much joy and love and is truly Daddy's Girl. Thank you both. You provide me with the constant purpose behind being free (and not tied to a time-stealing job) and you provide the joy of one adventure after another! I truly am blessed! To my dad, Bob Burley, with whom I have the longest of all relationships! Thank you for your love, loyalty, friendship and support

To my co-author and good friend Bryan Fergus I would like to say thank you for carrying the ball on many occasions while working on this project. A special thanks to Debi and your children for letting me "borrow" so much of your time to complete the book. And thank you for your knowledge, and expertise on the subject of personal development and psychology. Without your dedication and commitment we would still be working on this now completed book. Thanks for everything, Bryan.

I would like to thank my new Shield business partners: Joe Arlt (United States); Steve Dover (Australia); and Adrian Oakman (New Zealand) and their staffs. We are creating incredible things together. And The Shield's dedication to defending, protecting, and providing the regular person of Planet Earth with the opportunity to "own their own home" will benefit thousands for years to come. Thank you all for your integrity, honesty, loyalty and support. You truly are the best of the best from your own respective countries.

My associates at Burley & Associates, Inc. who are much more than just co-workers but are friends, confidants and invaluable in my life, I give a special thanks. To Bob Burley (My Father and Field Manager); Cindy Chapin (Logistics Manager and Product Creation); Bryan Fergus (Co-Author, Product Creation, and Spiritual Advisor); Jordan Holmes (General Office); Sue Holmes (Logistics and Office Administration); Regina Redmond (Office Manager and Real Estate Operations); Tyrone Thomas (IP Support); and Chad Watson (National Investment Specialist for the Shield). Thank you, you are the greatest team ever.

I would like to thank all of my investors for their belief, trust and support over the many years.

I would like to thank the people of integrity that I am fortunate enough to call friends and do business with for these many years: Al Allen, Cheri Hill, and the entire staff at Sage International (US Entity and Tax Strategies); Keith Cunningham (Business Strategy and Negotiations); Stephanie Olsen (Financial Planning and Shield Investor Relations); Kevin Stock of Image Support (Cover Design); Jeffrey Taylor (Real Estate Landlording); Dr. Van Tharp (Psychology and Investing); Don Wolfe (Mastery Training).

To my great friends and Australian promoters, Suzi Dafnis, Peter Johnston, and Sue Price of Pow Wow Events International, my sincere thanks for your trust and support in my work. And a special thanks to your incredible team.

To my dear friends John and Debbie McCants (Real Estate Investing and Public Speaking). Your friendship and support is incredible. Thanks for always being there.

To the greatest training staff in the World, bar none. Each and everyone of these outstanding people are Burley Boot Camp Graduates who then made the leap of faith to become an Advanced Investor in their own right. Together they have completed thousands of transactions. To the volunteer trainers at the Burley Boot Camp who are so truly dedicated to helping others create Powerful Changes for themselves. I salute you:

Darla and Perry Anderson, Joe Arlt, Troy Arment, Gil Barden, Tony Barton, John Black, Roslyn and Wayne Bourke, Bob Burley, John Burley, Jr., Shari Burley, Carol Caldwell, Matthew Chan, Craig Chandler, Cindy Chapin, Steve Copper, Tony Dean, Sandra

Dignam, Steve Dover, Dean Edelson, Bryan Fergus, Marleen Geyen, Bill Gordon, Simon Hall, Felicity Heffernan, Gina and Mike Hinds, Jerry and Lisa Hoganson, Sue Holmes, Greg Hooper, Melita Hunt, Hymer, Tami Iredale, Leonie Jackson, Damion Lupo, Sylvia Lundsford, Troy Mann, CJ Mathews, John and Debbie McCants, Scott Nash, Valera Peterson, Michael Pettett, Donovan Pieterese, Richard Portakiewicz, Adrian Oakman, Jim Sheils, Brad Simmons, Clinton Swaine, Harriet Trussell, Glen Warren, Chad Watson, Shawn Whetten, Bruce Whiting and all of their families.

To the many others who have supported myself and my works including:

Matthew Chan (www.mastermindforum.com), the Downie Family, Tony Edward, Graeme Fowler, Simon Hall, Dan and Janice Osborne, Kelly and Anna Ritchie, Peter Aranyi and Pearl Sidwell, Jackie Sourry, Richard and Veronica Tan, Bellum and Doreen Tan, Tyrone Thomas, Bruce Whiting, the Staff at the Embassy Suites which is home for Burley Boot Camp.

To all my thousands of graduates both past and present, thank you for your support and your continued success. The changes that I have witnessed in your lives have made me so proud. I look forward to continuing to hear about your many triumphs and successes.

My sincerest thanks and best wishes,
John Burley

Bryan's Acknowledgements

Writing *Powerful Changes*! has been an amazing experience. I am so thankful to two separate groups of people for the support and encouragement they have offered during the writing of this book. First, I want to thank the people who shared so much of their personal lives with me. This book represents countless hours of conversations with some of the most inspiring people in the world. These people generously opened up the pages of their lives and allowed me to ask them some intensely personal questions in an effort to understand the process they went through as they journeyed toward lives of meaning and fulfillment. I am eternally grateful to everyone who participated in these interviews. Your willingness to be involved and your openness during your interviews have made this book a helpful tool that will allow countless people to live better lives. Thank you all so very much.

Second, I want to thank all of the people who empowered me to coauthor *Powerful Changes*! This book truly represents their unfailing encouragement and the generous investments they have made in my personal life. I have been able to co-author this book in large part due to the insight and wisdom that I have gained from these friends. I feel the need to thank some of them by name. I would like to thank John Burley, my very close friend and partner in empowering people to make Powerful Changes, for the privilege of co-authoring this book with him. I would also like to thank my true and trusted friend, Mark Martin, for his constant support and loyal companionship as I have walked the path of my own personal journey toward a changed life. I also want to thank a remarkable and truly insightful woman named Cinthia Hiett who has helped me realize my potential to make positive changes in my own life and has been a constant believer in my ability to soar to new heights as I continue to grow as a human being.

Foremost, I want to thank my beautiful wife, Debi, for the extra support and encouragement she has given me during the writing of this book. Debi has been my constant companion throughout my personal Powerful Changes Process. Knowing Debi has made me a better man than I ever would have been without her. Debi, thank you for filling my life with laughter, smiles, happiness and joy. And thank you for reminding me that the most important things in life really aren't "things" at all. I also want to thank my three beautiful children – Tristen, Tess, and Timothy – for putting up with my writing schedule and always being ready to play with me at the drop of a hat. Tristen, Tess, and Timothy – I can't stop smiling when I'm with all of you. Thank you for doing that to me.

Most importantly, I want to thank the God of the Universe for being my Heavenly Father, Faithful Friend, Sympathetic Comforter, and Tender Teacher. "You have pleaded my soul's cause; You have redeemed my life". (Lamentations 3:58). Thank You so much.

We both want to thank the entire Burley Boot Camp family for their willingness to participate in this project. You are amazing people who truly give of yourselves to make life better for thousands of people. You are heroes that deserve to be admired. We admire you and are very proud of all the changes you have made in your lives.

We also want to specifically thank the people who have given us permission to use their stories in this important book. Joe Arlt, John McCants, Adrian Oakman, Steve Dover, Craig Chandler, Gil Barden, Felicity Heffernan, Dean Edelson, John Black, and Jerry Hoganson – thank you all for sacrificing some of your personal privacy in an effort to make life better for countless people. You are amazing and generous people. We know that this record of your real-life stories is a fitting tribute to the Powerful Changes that you have made. Our sincerest thanks and blessings go to each and every one of you.

John Burley's Level 5

Advanced Investing Boot Camp

John Burley and his team of real estate experts conduct the world famous Level 5 Advanced Investing Boot Camp several times a year. This event is completely prepares YOU to create success by becoming a knowledgeable and confident real estate investor.

John masterfully combines a classroom setting with hands on field work to create a learning environment that has never been seen anywhere in the world.

In this five-day program, you will have the opportunity to work with some of the most successful investors in the world today. These investors agree to come and work with you, to share their knowledge and experience, as their opportunity to give back what they have learned. Why, you might ask? It is our philosophy that there is no such thing as Scarcity-- only Prosperity! Therefore, it is our DUTY to share our knowledge and experience.

To receive our informational package about Boot Camp which includes a video tape, CD and brochure, contact: In Australia and New Zealand Pow Wow Events International: 1300 550 240 or +(61) 2 9662 8488; E-mail: burley@powwowevents.com.au
In the USA, Canada and Internationally: Prosperity Training, Inc. 1800 561 8246, International +1 (623) 561 8246.

Investor Resource Materials

Thank you for reading Powerful Changes. On these pages are details of John Burley's and Bryan Fergus's unique learning resources that have been designed to give you additional investment education.

Winning the Money Game

This live recording of a three-day seminar is the most revealing ever done on the subject of money. Information covered includes: The Seven Money Habits; The Levels of Investor; How the 'normal' person can become debt-free in 3-7 years (including your home and cars); Where to invest your money today and how to keep and protect your assets. Learn John's insider investment strategies. Develop a personal financial system designed to reduce debt and expenses while providing for long term financial security.

> 12 audio tapes – US $299.00
> AUD $429.00

Make Fortunes in Foreclosures

This is how John acquired 152 properties using NONE of his own money. Each and every one of these properties produces Positive Cash Flow. Most experts agree that this is the #1 program for the real estate investor to begin their career. Recorded in the studio, this program teaches you the Eight Principles of Real Estate Investing. Learn the 'Nuts and Bolts' of how to invest and remarket foreclosures.

> 4 audio tapes plus workbook – US $149.00
> AUD $210.00

All prices are in US and Australian dollars (AUD include GST)
In Australia/New Zealand order now by calling 1300 550 240 or +(61) 2 9662 8448
or visit www.powwowevents.com.au
In the US order now by calling 1 800 561 8246 or visit: www.johnburley.com

Blueprint for Success Real Estate Program

The success rate of students attending this five-day real estate training is four times greater than the industry average. It was this training that led Robin Leach of Lifestyles of the Rich and Famous fame to proclaim John Burley as one of the Premier Investors in America. Learn how to buy and resell real estate for Quick Cash (us$10,000+) within 90 days from completion of the training. Systems for developing long term cash flow are covered in great detail.

20 audio tapes – US $399.00

AUD$645.00

Or manual (200+ pages) – US $99.00

AUD$135.00

Secrets of The Professional Investor

Did you know nine out of ten investors do not make much money, if any? John Burley and Robert Kiyosaki show you how to be an unbeatable investor who wins consistently. In this tape set (recorded in Sydney), they speak frankly on how to make large sums of money with minimal risk. What is more, they candidly reveal how much investors are lied to, often by people they trust. Get the hard facts on how you can get on the fast track to wealth... and if you want, retire early.

16 audio tapes – US $299.00

AUD$429.00

All prices are in US and Australian dollars (AUD include GST)
In Australia/New Zealand order now by calling 1300 550 240 or +(61) 2 9662 8448
or visit www.powwowevents.com.au
In the US order now by calling 1 800 561 8246 or visit: www.johnburley.com

Infinite Wealth

What is Infinite Wealth? What would it mean to you to be Infinitely Wealthy? How can you achieve Infinite Wealth? In this tape series John R. Burley and Dr. Van K. Tharp along with Stephanie Olsen and Ken Long help you to answer these questions. The processes of making money and accumulating significant wealth, including millionaire status, are very easy. They could be taught to every child in school by the third grade. Unfortunately, these principles are not taught in most schools or even in our universities. Instead, most school systems teach us biases which prevent people from making money and even hinders us from having a successful, happy life. This three day workshop was recorded "Live" and was designed to teach you how easy it is to be "Infinitely Wealthy".

12 audio tapes plus manual – US $299.00

AUD$429.00

Spirituality of Wealth

In The Spirituality Of Wealth, Bryan Fergus will help you understand the important connection between your inner spiritual life and your daily financial practices. While some people teach that you must choose between being spiritually aware and financially prosperous, Bryan helps you see that you can experience both spiritual and financial abundance. By taking an honest look at the ancient sacred texts that have shaped popular spiritual perceptions of wealth, you will discover how ancient wisdom can actually help you get the most out of your money. Bryan shares the insights he has gained from his years of experience as a Spiritual Director as well as his extensive education to help you develop a spiritually sensitive approach to becoming financially prosperous. This series will give you the insights you need to live a spiritually abundant life while you move toward personal financial freedom.

6 audio tapes plus manual – US $199.00

AUD$225.00

All prices are in US and Australian dollars (AUD include GST)
In Australia/New Zealand order now by calling 1300 550 240 or +(61) 2 9662 8448
or visit www.powwowevents.com.au
In the US order now by calling 1 800 561 8246 or visit: www.johnburley.com

Investor Resource

Materials

As a way of saying 'thankyou' for reading this book and increasing your knowledge about financial success, we make available to you an audio cassette tape entitled:

"The 7 Levels of Investor"

Call Australia/New Zealand
1300 550 240 or +(61) 2 9662 8488
USA 1-(800) 561 8246
Outside USA 1-(623) 561 8246

See John Burley Live

John Burley visits Australia and New Zealand regularly to present his Winning the Money Game and Automatic Wealth programs. He also presents at his Level 5 Advanced Investing Boot Camp in Phoenix, AZ USA. John is an excellent educator who demystifies the subject of money and investment.

For information about John's events in Australia and New Zealand, and his Advanced Investing Boot Camp held in Phoenix, Arizona USA, contact: Pow Wow Events International on 1300 550 240 or +(61) 2 9662 8488 or visit: www.powwowevents.com.au
In the USA, Canada and internationally, contact: Prosperity Training on 1 800 561 8246 or visit: www.johnburley.com